Colossians
Verse-by-Verse

Colossians
Verse-by-Verse

Steve Lewis

Bible Study Companion Series:

Colossians Verse-by-Verse

Steve Lewis

This work is licensed under CC BY-ND 4.0.
To view a copy of this license, visit
http://creativecommons.org/licenses/by-nd/4.0/

Unless otherwise noted, Bible quotations are taken from the New American Standard Bible®, Copyright © 1960, 1962, 1963, 1968, 1971, 1972, 1973, 1975, 1977, 1995 by The Lockman Foundation. Used by permission. (www.Lockman.org)

Cover image by Laela on Unsplash.com

Contents

Introduction to Colossians
Colossians 1:1-2 3

Paul's Thanks and Prayer for Spiritual Maturity
Colossians 1:3-14 13

The Greatness of Christ
Colossians 1:15-23 27

Paul's Passion for the Church
Colossians 1:24-2:5 45

Walk in the Riches of Christ
Colossians 2:6-15 61

Wrong Ways to Master the Flesh
Colossians 2:16-23 79

Detour ~ the "Colossian Heresy" 90

Right Ways to Master the Flesh (Part One)
Colossians 3:1-10 99

Right Ways to Master the Flesh (Part Two)
Colossians 3:11-17 121

In Christ at Home
Colossians 3:18-4:6 141

Paul's Companions
Colossians 4:7-18 161

Reference Abbreviations

Barnes	Albert Barnes, *Notes on the Bible*, e-Sword.
BKC	*The Bible Knowledge Commentary* (Victor Books, 1983).
Boyer	James L. Boyer, *For a World Like Ours* (BMH, 1971).
Carson	Herbert M. Carson, *Colossians & Philemon* (Eerdmans, 1977).
Constable	Thomas Constable, *Notes on Colossians* (2023), https://planobiblechapel.org/tcon/notes/pdf/colossians.pdf
DPT	Mal Couch, ed., *Dictionary of Premillennial Theology* (Kregel Publications, 1996).
Erickson	Millard J. Erickson, *Christian Theology* (Baker Book House, 1985).
Expositors	*Expositor's Bible Commentary,* e-Sword.
Fructenbaum	Arnold Fructenbaum, *Footsteps of the Messiah* (Ariel Ministries, 2003).
Guzik	*David Guzik's Enduring Word Commentary*, e-Sword.
Harrison	Everett F. Harrison, *Colossians: Christ All-Sufficient* (Moody Press, 1971).
Hooker	Morna D. Hooker, "Were there False Teachers in Colossae?" *Christ and Spirit in the New Testament*, Lindars and Smalley, ed. (Cambridge Press, 1973).
House	H. Wayne House, "Heresies in the Colossian Church," *Bibliotheca Sacra* 149 (Jan 1992).
ISBE	*International Standard Bible Encyclopedia*, e-Sword.
JFB	Robert Jamieson, A.R. Fausset, David Brown, *Commentary on the Whole Bible*, e-Sword.
MacArthur	John MacArthur, *Colossians and Philemon* (Moody Publishers, 1992).
Meyer	F. B. Meyer, *Through the Bible Day by Day*, e-Sword.
Pentecost	J. Dwight Pentecost, *Designed to be Like Him* (Discovery House: 1994).
Pulpit	*The Pulpit Commentary*, e-Sword.
RWP	A. T. Robertson, *Word Pictures in the New Testament*, e-Sword.
Ryrie-B	Charles C. Ryrie, *Balancing the Christian Life* (Moody Press, 1994).
Ryrie-T	Charles C. Ryrie, *Basic Theology* (Moody Press, 1999).
Thayer	Joseph Thayer, *Greek-English Lexicon of the New Testament* (Hendrickson, 1996).
Vincent	Marvin R. Vincent, *Vincent's Word Studies*, e-Sword.
Wiersbe	Warren W. Wiersbe, *The Bible Exposition Commentary: Vol 2* (Victor Books, 1989).
Woods	Andrew M. Woods, *The Coming Kingdom* (Grace Gospel Press, 2016).
ZNBC	*Zondervan NIV Bible Commentary, Vol 2: New Testament* (Zondervan Publishing House, 1994).
Zodhiates	Spiros Zodhiates, *The Complete Word Study Dictionary* (AMG Publishers, 1992).
Zuck	Roy B. Zuck, *Basic Bible Interpretation* (Victor Books, 1991).

Preface to the Bible Study Companion Series

Bible study is such an important activity because knowing and doing the will of God depends on an accurate understanding of His written Word. The obedient Christian life is based on the assumption that believers know the truth about what they are to obey. God has not been silent, and He has not left us without detailed instructions for living. We have God's complete revelation for us today in the Bible.

The Bible is a collection of writings that God directed and inspired men to write. It was recorded in the common languages that people used to communicate their ideas to each other. We must remember this as we study the Bible. The principles for Bible study follow the same rules we use every day to understand the meaning of any written communication.

As we study the Bible our goal should be to understand the message that the original text was intended to communicate. This means we are not allowed to make the Bible say what we want it to say. We must let the Bible speak for itself. The hard work of Bible study involves carefully examining the written text of Scripture in order to understand exactly what that text was intended to communicate.

Since the biblical authors used normal language, we must use the regular principles of grammar and sentence structure to understand the Bible's message. Scripture was not written in some secret code that requires a hidden formula to decipher. Instead it was written in the common languages of the people who lived during those times (Hebrew, Aramaic, and Greek). For that reason, this Bible Study Companion contains many references to the words, grammar, and sentence structure of the original languages. This is necessary because most of us are not familiar with the ways that ancient writers communicated, and these insights will help us to clearly understand their message.

We must also remember that the biblical writings were recorded at specific times in human history. They were written to specific readers in specific historical, geographical, and cultural situations. In order to understand the purpose and message of the Bible, we must also study the history, geography, and culture of the original writers and readers. The meaning of each biblical expression is influenced and even determined by the context in which it was written. As one scholar has said,

> Just as we may be puzzled by the way people do things in other countries, so we may be puzzled by what we read in the Bible. Therefore it is important to know what the people in the Bible thought, believed, said, did, and made. To the extent we do this we are able to comprehend it better and communicate it more accurately. If we fail to give attention to these matters of culture, then we may be guilty of reading into the Bible our own ideas. [Zuck, 79]

This Bible Study Companion will provide help as you go through the text of the Bible just as it was written, in a verse-by-verse manner. Since the original text was written and read in successive order, this companion guide will include definitions, concepts, and ideas that will help you to understand the meaning of the phrases and sentences in the order in which they unfold. It is our prayer that God will guide and direct your study of His Word so that you will experience the rich blessings that come from studying the Bible.

Introduction to Colossians

(Colossians 1:1-2)

As we study the book of Colossians in the New Testament, our goal is to understand its message and the principles which believers today can use to increase their devotion to Jesus Christ and to live lives that are worthy of His calling.

I don't know about you, but sometimes when I turn to a book like Colossians, it seems like I am reading someone else's mail. That is partly because the book of Colossians *is a letter* that was written by someone almost 2000 years ago. So not only are we attempting to understand what we might call an "antique" piece of correspondence, but we are looking at an English translation of that letter which was originally written in the Greek language. In addition to the language gap, we are seeing descriptions of people, places, and events that happened in a foreign land which was quite a different culture and environment from our own.

But just as we would handle any letter (whether ancient or modern), we need to determine what message the author of this letter intended to communicate. We are not free to interpret the author's words any way we want to, because it is the author's intended meaning that we need to understand. This is exactly the same approach that the original readers of this letter would have taken, and it is the common approach today for understanding any type of communication. These words were written by a real person to other real people who were in a situation where they needed to hear an important message with some relevant information that would help them to handle their circumstances. With that being said, let's dig into the book of Colossians.

Col 1:1 – Paul, an apostle of Jesus Christ by the will of God, and Timothy our brother,

One of the first things we notice about this letter is that the format is different from letters we may write today. In ancient times letters would start with what we might call the signature – in other words, who was writing the letter. The signature would be followed by the address, or who were the intended recipients. Then there would be a salutation, an ascription of appreciation, and finally the body of the letter.

Paul gives his name as the author. So who was Paul? If your Bible has a subject index or a topical concordance, you can look him up and see many references to Paul starting in the Bible book of Acts, which is the historical account of the beginning days of the Church. The first reference is Acts 13:9 which says, "But Saul, who was also known as Paul, filled with the Holy Spirit, fixed his gaze on him." This tells us that Paul was formerly known as Saul, so a quick search starting in Acts 7:58 gives us an amazing account of who Saul was, how he came to trust in Christ for his own salvation, and how he became the man Paul who we see here writing the book of Colossians.

By Paul's own testimony (Phil 3:5-7) he was, "circumcised the eighth day, of the nation of Israel, of the tribe of Benjamin, a Hebrew of Hebrews; as to the Law, a Pharisee; as to zeal, a persecutor of the church; as to the righteousness which is in the Law, found blameless."

That is quite a pedigree from a Jewish perspective, but when Paul looked back on his so-called accomplishments during his youth, he considered himself "not fit to be called an apostle, because I persecuted the church of God. But by the grace of God I am what I am, and His grace toward me did not prove in vain" (1 Cor 15:9-10).

Later in his ministry when he defended his apostleship against attack by false teachers in the city of Corinth, Paul correctly claimed that he was not "in the least inferior to the most eminent apostles." Those false teachers were boasting of their qualifications, so Paul answered them in kind (see 2 Cor 11:22-28).

> "Are they Hebrews? So am I. Are they Israelites? So am I. Are they descendants of Abraham? So am I. Are they servants of Christ? I more so; in far more labors, in far more imprisonments, beaten times without number, often in danger of death. Five times I received from the Jews thirty-nine lashes. Three times I was beaten with rods, once I was stoned, three times I was shipwrecked, a night and a day I have spent in the deep. I have been on frequent journeys, in dangers from rivers, dangers from robbers, dangers from my countrymen, dangers from the Gentiles, dangers in the city, dangers in the wilderness, dangers on the sea, dangers among false brethren; I have been in labor and hardship, through many sleepless nights, in hunger and thirst, often without food, in cold and exposure. Apart from such external things, there is the daily pressure on me of concern for all the churches."

After telling us his name in Colossians, Paul then gives a brief description of himself.

Paul, an apostle of Jesus Christ = An apostle was an important office that was active during the early stages of the Church. It involved the work of laying the foundation for the New Testament Church and recording divinely inspired instructions for the Church Age. We know this because that is how the work of an apostle is described in 1 Cor 3:9-11 and Eph 2:19-22.

Paul, an apostle...by the will of God = Paul's apostleship was not of his own making or choosing, nor was he appointed by the Church – he was an apostle because God called him and set him apart for this office. You can read more about Paul's calling in the book of Acts where Paul repeats this story three times (chapters 9, 22, and 26). In order to be an apostle, one had to be called to that office by Jesus Himself, so beware when someone claims to be an apostle today. In 1 Corinthians 15 Paul explained how Jesus appeared to several people after His resurrection, then he said, "last of all, as to one untimely born, He appeared to me also" (1 Cor 15:8). Jesus confronted Paul and called him to be an apostle to the Gentiles. In Paul's own words: "For so the Lord has commanded us, 'I have placed you as a light for the Gentiles, that you may bring salvation to the end of the earth'" (Acts 13:47).

I would encourage you to learn more about this giant of the faith who is writing this letter. One Bible scholar went so far as to say that, apart from Jesus Christ Himself, the apostle Paul is the most important and influential person in history. Almost half of the New Testament books were written by Paul. By identifying himself as the apostle Paul he was establishing his authority for writing this letter to these people.

and Timothy our brother = In most of Paul's letters he would typically mention the name of someone who would be familiar to the intended audience. In this case Paul associates himself with Timothy in the heading of this letter. This does not mean that Timothy was the co-author of the letter, but that he was someone with Paul at the time he wrote the letter and someone who would have been respected by the readers. You can read more about Timothy's life and ministry starting in Acts 16.

Notice that Paul is an apostle, but Timothy is a brother. This tells us that once the foundation of the New Testament was completed by the apostles, there was no need for any more of them. The remaining work of building the Church was carried on by faithful brothers who ministered to the needs of the Church, and Timothy was a stellar example of such a brother.

Col 1:2 – To the saints and faithful brethren in Christ who are at Colossae: Grace to you and peace from God our Father.

In verse one we saw the author, and here in the first part of verse two the address is given – in other words, the recipients of the letter.

to the saints and faithful brethren = saints is the Greek word *hagioi* which could be translated "holy ones" or "ones who are set apart by God." This letter is addressed to believers in Jesus Christ whom God has set apart as His own special people.

These saints are further described as faithful brethren.

faithful is the Greek word *pistos* which could be translated as "believing" or as "faithful and steadfast." *pistos* carries the idea of "firmness in faith" or "fully trusting" and therefore trustworthy in their commitment to the Savior.

brethren or brothers indicates the close family relationship in the household of faith.

This letter was intended to be read by people who had heard the gospel message of salvation through the substitutionary death of Christ on our behalf and His resurrection. These people were fully trusting or relying on that truth for their eternal salvation. For a succinct statement of the gospel message, see Paul's earlier letter to the church at Corinth (1 Cor 15:3-4).

in Christ = If there were any doubt about the spiritual position of the recipients of this letter, we see that they are in Christ – because of their faith and trust in the work of Christ to purchase their salvation, the Holy Spirit has set them apart and placed them into the body of Christ. As Paul says later, their lives are "hidden with Christ in God" (Col 3:3). When God looks at the believer, He sees the righteousness of Christ.

These believers are spiritually **in Christ**, but they are physically located **at Colossae**. So where in the world was Colossae?

According to ancient sources, Colossae was one of the earliest and most important cities in the Lycus River valley, which is located in what today would be southwestern Turkey. It was in a region called Phrygia, and as early as 480 BC the Greek historian Herodotus referred to it as "a great city" on the established trade route between the Aegean Sea and the Euphrates River valley. Persian kings Xerxes and Cyrus the Younger both marched along this route during their military conquests. Around 400 BC the Greek historian Xenophon wrote that it was "a populous city, wealthy and large." But later in Roman times the commercial road was rerouted through the nearby city of Laodicea, so Colossae became what the Roman geographer Strabo called "a small town." One Bible commentator said that Colossae was the most unimportant town to which Paul ever wrote a letter.

In New Testament times its population consisted mainly of native Phrygians and Greek settlers, along with a number of Jewish colonists who came to the area around the time of Antiochus III in the second century BC.

In Paul's day Colossae was a small market town, focused mainly on produce such as olives and figs. The many sheep pastured in the area contributed to a wool industry which included the production of a popular wool dyed dark red or purple. In the first century AD, the Roman historian Pliny wrote about the purple wool that Colossae was famous for. It was made with a dye from the cyclamen flower, and the Latin word for purple wool ("collossinus") seems to be derived from the name of this city.

The native Phrygians had a tendency to emotional forms of religious expression with exciting music and frenzied dancing. There were many pagan Phrygian deities, but when

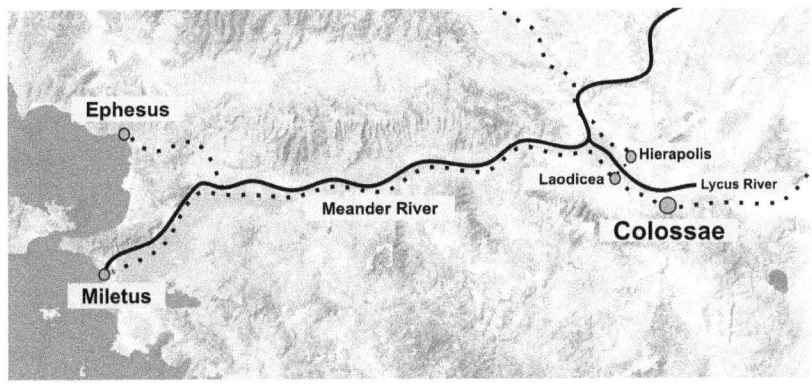

Rome imported the Phrygian rituals, many considered them too extreme and were not allowed to participate in them.

The area of the Lycus River valley is prone to earthquakes, and there was a major earthquake about AD 60. The important cities nearby were quickly rebuilt, but Colossae continued its decline. It was sparsely populated as the residents moved to the more prosperous commercial centers of Laodicea and Hierapolis just a few miles away.

Unlike many sites mentioned in the New Testament, the city of Colossae was not studied by archaeologists until very recently. There has been some preliminary investigation of the acropolis mound of ancient Colossae. A 5,000 seat amphitheater has been identified on its eastern slope, which may be located near the agora or marketplace next to the city's main north-south road. There are sections of columns in nearby fields, some of which may mark the location of an early church.

A cemetery has been found north of the Lycus River. There are two main types of burial monuments: Greek tombs with an outer room attached to an inner space, and tumuli which are underground tombs with stepped entrances from the surface that lead down to the place of burial. One Colossian burial monument dated to the late first century AD was discovered about a century ago in a nearby city, where it had

Building stones scattered in the ruins of the ancient city of Colossae.

been taken from the ancient site and put on display.

Closer to the Lycus River there are water channels which are visible. These were carved out of rock with complex sluice gates and pipes that allowed water to be diverted from the river for irrigation, washing, and commercial use. An early second century AD inscription on the base of a marble statue honors the repairer of Colossae's baths, showing that these pools were one of the city's important institutions.

Many Roman coins from Colossae show the name of the city, of Roman officials, and various gods including Artemis, Helios, Dionysis, Demos, Boule, Tyche, Isis, Serapis, and a local river god. The coins show that the typical Greek and Roman deities, plus local Phrygian gods, were worshiped in the region. Hopefully more information will be uncovered as the archaeological investigation continues. Colossae was largely abandoned by the 5th century AD, then it was attacked by Muslims in the 7th century AD, and it was totally destroyed in the 12th century AD.

So the evidence from archaeology and ancient manuscripts shows that Colossae was similar to other cities in Asia Minor during the Roman period. Greek was the main language, they issued their own coinage, and they lived according to typical Roman social customs. The people had families and servants, understood Greek, used Roman money, worshiped various deities, and worked primarily in agriculture. These are the people that Paul is writing to in Colossae.

In the last part of verse two we see the salutation of the letter. Today we might write, "Dear Sir" or (if we were addressing a family member) "Dearest Aunt Lucy". In Paul's time the salutation was often expressed using a form of the Greek word "rejoice" (*chairein*), which was used to mean: "May you be glad" or "I wish you well" or simply "Greetings."

Grace to you and peace from God our Father = Among the Jews the customary greeting was the Hebrew word *shalom*, "Peace." So the apostle Paul typically combines these two salutations in most of his letters. He used the Greek word *charis* (a form of the word *chairein*) that expresses the unmerited favor of God, which is His goodness toward those who cannot earn or do not deserve His favor. Then he added the Greek word for "peace" which expresses an inner harmony because of our restored relationship with God. Paul expressed it in the form of a wish or prayer: Grace to you and peace. Notice that the source and provider of these blessings is God our Father.

Think about the things we have seen so far in Colossians and ask yourself these questions:

– What is the status of your own faith?

– Would the apostle Paul consider you someone who is "set apart for God" – one who is fully trusting in Jesus for your personal salvation?

– If Paul were writing to you, could he address you as a brother in Christ?

If you're not sure, then you can fix that right now. Being a Christian means that you've learned about what Jesus did for you when He came to earth as a man to take the punishment which you rightfully deserve as you face a holy God. He voluntarily went to the cross to suffer and die in your place, and after paying the ultimate price for your sins and mine, He rose from his tomb on the third day.

Understand that you can know those facts but still not be a Christian. Jesus did this for you and freely offers you the gift of salvation and eternal life with Him, but you need to fully trust in what He did for you. The Bible talks about having faith or believing, and this means that you know what Jesus did for you, you accept that it is true, and you are completely relying on these truths for your eternal destiny. It seems simple, but it may be the most difficult decision you'll ever make. Simply acknowledge what Jesus did by dying for you and tell Him that you are trusting in that alone to reconcile you to God. It's the only hope that any of us have, and it's the most important step you can take in this life. As it says in the well-known verse John 3:16 – "For God so loved the world, that He gave His only begotten Son, that whoever believes in Him shall not perish, but have eternal life."

Paul's Thanks and Prayer for Spiritual Maturity

(Colossians 1:3-14)

As we saw in the last chapter, ancient letters would start with what we might call the signature followed by the address and a salutation. In this section we will see what's called the ascription of appreciation, where in this letter Paul gives thanks for several things he appreciates about the Colossian believers. In addition to Paul's gratefulness for these believers, he also gives us some important background information about them, as well as about the state of the Gospel in the early days of the Church. If you've studied any of Paul's letters before, you also won't be surprised to see quite a bit of theology sprinkled throughout this section, which is typical of how he writes. With this as our starting point, let's see how Paul expresses his appreciation for the Colossians.

Paul's Appreciation for the Colossians

Col 1:3 – We give thanks to God, the Father of our Lord Jesus Christ, praying always for you,

He begins by saying, "We give thanks." **We** is the apostle Paul and his ministry partners. We'll see a little later who this includes besides Paul and Timothy. They know quite a bit about the Colossians and are responsible for encouraging them spiritually.

Shortly Paul will tell us what he appreciates about the Colossians, but notice that he does not address his appreciation directly to them. Instead he gives thanks to God, the Father of our Lord Jesus Christ. Here God is the one whom the Lord Jesus Christ revealed to us as the Father when He said, "He who has seen Me has seen the Father" (John 14:9). **Father** emphasizes the personal family relationship believers have with God. He is the source of every good thing in the Colossians' lives. Paul says that he gives thanks to God as he is praying always for them. **Praying** is the Greek word *proseuchomai*, which is the typical word for bringing your thoughts and requests to God.

The word **always** in the original language is positioned between giving thanks and praying, so it could go with either of those actions. It would make sense to say, "always giving thanks when we pray for you" but you can certainly imagine a man like Paul being in constant prayer, so "praying always for you" also makes sense.

In this verse Paul mentions God the Father as well as God the Son, and a few verses later he will also mention God the Holy Spirit – so in this section of the letter we see the entire Trinity represented. In verse 3 Paul has said they were giving thanks, so in verse 4 he begins to tell us what they were thankful for.

Col 1:4 – since we heard of your faith in Christ Jesus and the love which you have for all the saints;

Notice first of all that Paul had only **heard** about the Colossians. Even though Paul carried out an intensive two-year ministry throughout the Roman province of Asia Minor (Acts 19:10), he apparently had not been to Colossae. Later in Col 2:1 Paul says that they had not seen his face, and the Greek word for **see** (*horao*) means "to look at" and by implication "to become personally acquainted with." Later we will find out more about the person who was likely responsible for sharing the gospel with the Colossians.

There are three main qualities which Paul is thankful for, and the first two are given in this verse. First, Paul is thankful for their faith in Christ Jesus. **Faith** is the Greek word *pistis* and, as we saw in the last chapter, faith is the firm conviction of the truth of something. The Colossians' faith is **in Christ Jesus**. The object of faith is crucially important. These people were trusting in the gospel message of salvation through the substitutionary death of Christ on our behalf and His resurrection. They were relying on that truth for their eternal destiny.

When a person puts their faith in Christ Jesus for salvation, there are dozens of things that God does for that person. They all happen behind the scenes and even without our being aware of them. The apostle Paul will mention several of these things in the coming verses, but we should understand that faith is the foundation on which everything else is built. One of the things that God provides is the ability for believers to love others unconditionally.

So second, Paul is thankful for the **love** which they have for all the saints. There are several different Greek words which can be translated into English as love, so we should find out exactly what kind of love Paul is talking about. Here the Greek word *agape* is used, which is the same word used to describe the kind of love that God Himself demonstrates. In another letter Paul tells us that "The fruit of the Spirit is love" (Gal 5:22), so it is the indwelling Holy Spirit in the life of a believer which enables him to demonstrate God's kind of unconditional love for others. This kind of love could be described as unmerited, unselfish, and sacrificial. Someone has said, "In the Christian life, faith is the root and love is the fruit."

The aspect of their love that was most noteworthy was their expression of unconditional love within the household of faith to other believers – as he says here, the love which you have **for all the saints**. Before Jesus went to the cross He told His disciples: "I am giving you a new commandment, that you love one another; just as I have loved you, that you also love one another. By this all people will know that you are My disciples: if you have love for one another." (John 13:34-35) Paul had heard that the Colossians were living out this commandment in a way that was evident to everyone.

The third thing Paul is thankful for is the **hope** exhibited by the Colossians.

Col 1:5 – because of the hope laid up for you in heaven, of which you previously heard in the word of truth, the gospel

Even though the church in Colossae may have been only a few years old, and these people may have been relatively new believers, they had been taught well about the basic truths of the faith. They understood that they had become mere pilgrims and strangers on this earth and that their true home is now with Christ. They had an eager expectation of this future life which they knew was laid up for them. Another of the things given to believers by God at the moment of salvation is a future with Him in heaven. The Greek word for the phrase **laid up** means to be stored away, or reserved and waiting for the arrival of the owner. Even though we may not see them here and now, there are many things that we have in Christ which are reserved for us and wait for our arrival in heaven to enjoy them. There is a glorious future awaiting the faithful.

To summarize, we could say that Paul is grateful for their **faith** in the past, which produced their **love** in the present, and that brought them **hope** for the future. One Bible commentator expressed it this way:

Faith is the soul looking upward to God; love looks outward to others; hope looks forward to the future. Faith rests on the past work of Christ; love works in the present; and hope anticipates the future. [BKC]

Starting in the last half of verse 5 Paul takes a short detour to describe what happened when the Colossians heard about the good news of what Christ Jesus did for them. The word **gospel** simply means good news. They had **previously heard** these truths about Christ in the **word of truth**. In order to become a believer and be reconciled to God, there is a message that you must understand. The words can be presented in any number of ways, but those who communicate the message must present the simple and straightforward truth about the work of Christ on our behalf. In today's world there are many people who wonder whether objective truth even exists, but the message of the gospel relies on the fact that there is such a thing as objective truth which can be communicated and understood by men, women, and children today. God's Word is truth (John 17:17), so we should saturate ourselves with the Scriptures in order to keep our focus on what is true. The proof that objective truth really does exist is seen in the very next verse.

Col 1:6 – which has come to you, just as in all the world also it is constantly bearing fruit and increasing, even as it has been doing in you also since the day you heard of it and understood the grace of God in truth;

Here Paul says that the Colossians themselves are proof that the gospel message is true and effective. The word of truth ... has come to you and is constantly bearing fruit. Lives are being changed for the better, and the positive fruit of godly living is evident not only in the Colossians but also in all the world. The gospel is a universal truth that was having this same effect everywhere it was being accepted as it spread across the known world of Paul's day. And God's work of reconciliation and renewal began in the Colossian believers immediately – as it says here, "since the day you heard and understood the message." The word **understood** is the Greek word *epignosis*, which means much more than simply knowing something. It carries the meaning of thoroughly understanding, of recognizing the importance, of accepting and applying something personally in your life. The Colossian believers placed all their faith and trust in the truth concerning the grace of God, which is the undeserved favor and blessing that comes to a believer as a result of Jesus Christ's death in our place as payment for your sins and mine, followed by His resurrection from the dead.

Col 1:7-8 – just as you learned it from Epaphras, our beloved fellow bond-servant, who is a faithful servant of Christ on our behalf, and he also informed us of your love in the Spirit.

The Greek word translated **learned** can carry the idea of gaining information, comprehending it, and then obeying it. These two verses tell us that a man named Epaphras brought the gospel to the Colossians. Later we see in Col 4:12 that he himself was from Colossae, and as it says here, he was working on Paul's behalf when he took the gospel message back to his hometown. Here Paul describes him as a **beloved fellow bondservant**. It is obvious that Paul has great affection and respect for Epaphras in his service for Christ. We know from Paul's letter to Philemon which accompanied the Colossian letter, that Epaphras had remained with Paul, who was under house arrest in Rome when he wrote these letters (Philemon 1:23).

Previously we saw that Paul commended the Colossians for their love for all the saints, and here we see that it was Epaphras who told Paul about the conditions of the church in Colossae. And he says that their unconditional, sacrificial love for the brethren was motivated and empowered through God the Holy Spirit.

This is where Paul ends the letter's ascription of appreciation, and now we'll see that Paul records a prayer for the Colossians starting in verse 9. The content of this prayer reflects the things that Paul heard were needed by the church at Colossae.

Paul's Prayer for Spiritual Maturity

In verses 3-4 Paul had said that ever since he heard of their faith, hope, and love, he had poured out his gratitude to God for them in his prayers. Here in verse 9 Paul gives specific details about his prayer requests for the Colossians.

Col 1:9 – For this reason also, since the day we heard of it, we have not ceased to pray for you and to ask that you may be filled with the knowledge of His will in all spiritual wisdom and understanding,

First, he asks that they may be filled with the **knowledge** of God's will. Every believer needs to know who God is and what He expects of us. The word knowledge here is not the normal Greek word for knowledge (*gnosis*). Instead Paul uses the same Greek word we saw in verse 6, which intensifies the meaning. *epignosis* means "thoroughly understanding, recognizing the importance, accepting and applying something personally in our lives."

Here Paul explains that he wants them to be **filled** with knowledge. This is the Greek word *pleroo* which means to completely fill to capacity, and maybe even beyond capacity by pressing down and cramming in as much as possible. This is the first time in this letter that we see one of the key words of the book of Colossians, which is filled or fullness. Remember that it means completely filled to capacity with nothing lacking.

But Paul isn't finished describing the quality of the knowledge he wants them to have. He continues by saying that their knowledge should be in "all spiritual wisdom and understanding." Not only does he desire that God give them a complete knowledge of His will, but he wants the Colossians to use or apply that knowledge with the utmost wisdom and understanding by the power of the indwelling Holy Spirit of God. **Wisdom** is the Greek word *sophia*, which some have described as "the ability to apply knowledge correctly." **Understanding** is the Greek word *sunesis*, which literally means "flowing together." So it is a mental "putting together" of ideas and actions to gain the best result in every situation. This is a very important prayer request for the Colossians, and it's one which will help to protect them from errors in their own thinking as well as from attacks by false teachers who may be trying to derail them.

In verse 9 Paul described the kind of in-depth knowledge of God that he is requesting for them, and then in verse 10 he describes how the right kind of knowledge will demonstrate itself in the believers' normal habits of daily life.

Col 1:10 – so that you will walk in a manner worthy of the Lord, to please Him in all respects, bearing fruit in every good work and increasing in the knowledge of God;

The word translated **walk** is the Greek word *peripateo* which is typically used to mean "daily walk and life or lifestyle." Paul is saying that the more they know about God's will and His ways, the more they will be able to live lives that are worthy of God and pleasing to Him. What we believe will affect how we behave. True spiritual wisdom always affects our daily life.

Here he tells us how we can determine whether we are handling our knowledge in the right way. We will live in a way that pleases God and will be fruitful in good works. You probably know of some Christians who seem to have lots of knowledge, but they are not living very attractive or fruitful lives. Unfortunately, it is possible for a believer to live like that, but we need to make every effort to avoid that for ourselves. Paul says if we gain godly knowledge and we demonstrate that knowledge in a pleasing and productive lifestyle, then God is able to increase our knowledge even more. If we show that we can handle more knowledge appropriately, then the cycle will continue.

The sequence we see here describes the process of growing in spiritual maturity, and that is what Paul is praying for the Colossians. With a foundation of faith in Christ Jesus, believers begin to grow in their knowledge and understanding of God and His will, which leads to living in a way that pleases God and grows into productive service for God. You can't snap your fingers and achieve complete spiritual maturity in an instant. Growth takes time and patient care.

The goal of a believer's life should be to glorify and please God. But, like many of you, most of the time I feel very inadequate in my own strength to live my life in the way Paul describes here. So next, Paul is going to tell us what resources God provides that can empower us to live this kind of pleasing and productive life.

Col 1:11 – strengthened with all power, according to His glorious might, for the attaining of all steadfastness and patience; joyously

Here Paul tells us about the power that is available to us. We do not need to rely only on our own strength to live a life that is worthy of God. Paul says we can be strengthened with all power. The Greek word for **power** is *dunamis*, which means inherent power or ability that arises from the nature of something. The English word dynamite comes from this term. The phrase **strengthened with all power** is literally "powered with all power" because the verb and noun in this phrase are both from the same root word.

But where does this extra power come from? Paul says it is according to His glorious might. Since God the Holy Spirit indwells every believer from the moment of salvation, He is able to energize us even when we seem to have very little strength of our own. We are still responsible for exercising our own strength of will and character, but the indwelling Spirit can energize us with all the strength and ability we need. We must rely on Him to energize us as we attempt to live our lives in the way God desires.

Paul ends this verse by describing two instances when we might need this godly inner strength. First, he says it is for "attaining all steadfastness." **Steadfastness** is the Greek word *hupomone* which literally means "to abide under." It could be translated as "patiently enduring difficult circumstances." When your situation or circumstances look grim, that is when you need to exhibit steadfastness. **Patience** is the Greek word *makrothumia* which literally means "long tempered." It can be translated as "longsuffering or forbearance toward people." So here we see that God can assist us whether we are dealing with difficult circumstances or with difficult people.

The final word in this verse tells us how we should react when dealing with the things that God brings to us in life. **Joyously** is from the same Greek word (*chara*) that was typically used in the salutation of ancient letters. It means "with gladness, cheerfulness, or joy." One Bible scholar expressed the importance of joy this way:

> Endurance and long-suffering are tremendous assets; but when they are accompanied by joyfulness, they reveal their supernatural character. [Harrison, 29]

It's possible for us to handle difficult circumstances or difficult people, but it's only when we do it with cheerfulness that it brings glory to God.

Col 1:12 – giving thanks to the Father, who has qualified us to share in the inheritance of the saints in Light.

Here we also see that **giving thanks** to God is an essential quality as we deal with the ups and downs of life. It may seem counterintuitive to thank God for difficult things in our lives, but when we do that, we are acknowledging that every situation of life is in His hands and under His control. It's easier to thank God for the good things, but it's when we affirm God's sovereignty over the difficult things that we prove we really understand who He is and what He is doing in our lives.

Paul now ends his prayer for the Colossians by mentioning something that God will provide for us in the future, as well as something that God has done for us in the past.

First, God qualified us to **share in the inheritance of the saints in Light**. The moment someone puts their faith in the person and work of Christ for salvation, God gives them a share in the heavenly realm that will be theirs when Christ returns for those who are His. Just as we know in earthly or legal terms, an heir is someone who has been granted an inheritance. Even though they do not currently possess their inheritance, they know that it's guaranteed by right. This is the concept that Paul shares in this verse. We each were qualified or made sufficient for this heavenly inheritance which all of the believing saints will possess in the future. This inheritance is described as being in the glorious light of God, which contrasts with the darkness that Paul is going to explain in the next two verses.

Col 1:13-14 – For He rescued us from the domain of darkness, and transferred us to the kingdom of His beloved Son, in whom we have redemption, the forgiveness of sins.

Here Paul tells us several of the things that God did for us in the past. These happen all at once at the point in time when a person trusts Christ for salvation. In contrast to the inheritance in light that Paul described previously, there is also a dark domain from which God rescued each of us. **Domain** is the Greek word *exousia* which means a realm of power and authority that rules over us. We were held captive and kept in bondage within this dark domain until God rescued us.

Paul expresses this transaction in two ways – stating both the negative and positive aspects of what Christ accomplished for us. First, God rescued us out of the power and sphere of the dark domain. **Rescued** is the Greek word *rhuomai* which means "to draw or pull something to oneself." God reached in and grabbed each one of us, pulling us out toward Himself. Second, Paul gives the positive side – God transferred us into His kingdom. **Transferred** is the Greek word *metestēsen*. It sounds similar to our English word "metastasis" and it means "to move from one state or place to another." God not only pulled us out of a dark place of bondage, but He brought us into a state of freedom and light, represented by the kingdom of His dear Son.

So does this verse teach that Christ's kingdom is a present reality for believers during the Church Age? The context of this passage gives us the answer. Just as God made us legal heirs of our heavenly inheritance, which we will ultimately possess in the future according to Col 1:12, so He also guaranteed our legal status as members of Christ's future kingdom – even though we will not actually experience the kingdom until our ultimate return to reign with Him during the millennial kingdom. One Bible scholar expressed it this way:

> While believers are legally heirs of God's kingdom, the kingdom is not yet a factual reality upon the earth. ... Paul wrote the book of Colossians at the same time as his other prison letters including Philippians and Ephesians. In Philippians believers are

called "citizens of heaven" (Phil 3:20). In Ephesians believers are said to be "seated with Christ in the heavenly places" (Eph 2:6). This heavenly position represents the legal standing of the believer. Yet believers are not actually in heaven now. ... Although believers may have been delivered legally from Satan's authority (1 John 5:18), they have not been delivered in fact and in present experience from Satan's authority. Rather believers regularly wrestle against Satan's authority. Ephesians 6:12 states, "For our struggle is not against flesh and blood, but against the rulers, against the powers, against the world forces of this darkness." ... The word translated "powers" is the Greek word *exousia*, which is the same word translated "domain" in Colossians 1:13. ... As is the case with both our redemption and freedom from Satanic authority, believers are legally and positionally citizens of a kingdom that will not be manifested upon the earth until a future time period. [Woods, 301-303]

In the last phrase of verse 14 Paul cannot resist mentioning another of the things that God accomplished for us through the death and resurrection of Christ. He says that in His beloved Son we have **redemption**. This is the powerful Greek word *apolutrōsis*, which means "to pay the ransom price for a slave or debtor in order to secure their release."

In addition to our redemption in Christ, we also have the forgiveness of sins. The Greek word **have** carries the meaning "to have and to hold; to own or possess." Just like our inheritance discussed previously, this is something that believers are guaranteed because of Christ's work on our behalf. First we saw God "buying back" our lives, and here we see Him "sending away" our sins. **Forgiveness** literally means "sending away" and providing freedom or release. The Greek word for **sin** here is the word *hamartiōn*, which means "to do wrong or to go wrong; to miss or wander from the path of righteousness." Unfortunately, this is the status of everyone who is under the influence of the domain of darkness. But God through Christ has provided an opportunity for freedom, which is given to every believer at the point when they put their trust in Christ's work on their behalf.

In light of all that believers have received from God, no wonder Paul tells us to give thanks for everything He has done for us. Paul gives us a wonderful example in this letter – even in the midst of very difficult circumstances, he was constantly praying with thankfulness and joy. How is your prayer life? What steps can you take that might make you even more productive in prayer?

What changes should we make in our lives that would allow God to fill us with the knowledge of His will? Are there distractions we should eliminate, or are there some activities we should make more of a priority? Once God provides more knowledge, are we putting it into practice by living lives that please the Lord and are productive for His work? Let us correctly handle the knowledge we have been given, so that we might be eligible to receive more understanding and discernment from God.

Right now, is there an area of your life which you are having a difficult time handling in your own strength? If so, commit that area to God and ask for His strength to help you.

If you want a list of some of the things for which you can thank God in your prayers, how about adding these from this section of Colossians:

– the hope laid up for me in heaven
– the fact that God's Word is true
– gratitude for my "Epaphras" – the one who shared the gospel with me
– help in dealing with difficult circumstances or difficult people
– thankfulness for my inheritance with the saints in light
– my rescue from the dark domain and membership in Christ's kingdom
– my redemption – the ransom price has been paid by Christ
– forgiveness of sins because of what Christ accomplished for me

The Greatness of Christ

(Colossians 1:15-23)

In the last chapter, we saw Paul say that God the Father "rescued us from the domain of darkness, and transferred us to the kingdom of His beloved Son, in whom we have redemption, the forgiveness of sins." His first emphasis was on the work of God the Father, but he ended by explaining the work of God the Son, Christ Jesus. So in this next section of Paul's letter to the Colossians the focus shifts exclusively to the Lord Jesus Christ.

Paul just finished telling us in the previous verses that spiritual knowledge, wisdom, and understanding are crucial for our growth toward Christian maturity, so now Paul proceeds to explain one of the most important things that believers must add to their knowledge. What we will cover today is one of the key passages in all of Scripture that describes who Jesus Christ is and what He does. If believers have a clear understanding of the greatness of Christ, then they will have a firm foundation of spiritual knowledge upon which to build their lives in a way that is pleasing to God. First, we see the greatness of Christ as the image of God.

The Greatness of Christ as the Image of God

Col 1:15a – He is the image of the invisible God,

He refers back to the Father's Beloved Son mentioned in verses 13-14. He is the same one who redeemed us, provided forgiveness of our sins, and into whose future kingdom believers will be welcomed. The subject of our study in this passage is the person and work of the Lord Jesus Christ. In theological terms, this is the study of Christology. So, take a deep breath and buckle your seatbelt because the apostle Paul is going to take us on a deep dive into the theology of Christ in the next few verses of Colossians.

We see in Col 1:15 that Christ is the **image of the invisible God**. These few simple words communicate a deep spiritual truth. Just to be clear here, God does not need an image of any kind. God knows perfectly without any helps or props or object lessons. However, from a human perspective, we do need help in order to see and understand something about the nature and character of God. We require a visual aid, and Jesus is that visual aid which we need.

Image is the Greek word *eikōn* which means a visual representation of something. In Greek thought an image shared in reality what it represents, so the word carries the idea of both representation and manifestation.

Why do we need this? As it says here, the reason is because God the Father by His very nature is invisible. In John 4:24 Jesus stated that "God is spirit." This means that He is not composed of matter and does not have physical substance. Therefore, He is not limited, for example, to a particular geographical location, and His nature cannot be destroyed as physical matter can. It's almost impossible for us to grasp this truth about the nature of God, and that is why the Lord Jesus Christ came in human flesh to show us the nature and character of God. One theologian expressed it this way:

> Jesus Christ is our best source for knowledge of deity. We assume that we know what God is really like. But it is in Jesus that God is most fully revealed and known. As John 1:18 says, "No one has ever seen God; the only Son, who is in the bosom of the Father, he has made him known." Thus our picture of what deity is like comes primarily through the revelation of God in Jesus Christ. ...

Sometimes we approach the incarnation with an assumption that it is virtually impossible. We know what humanity is and what deity is, and they are by definition incompatible. They are the finite and the infinite. But our understanding of human nature has been formed by looking at ourselves and the other humans around us. None of us represents humanity as it came from God's hand. Humanity was spoiled and corrupted by the sin of Adam and Eve. Consequently, we are not true human beings, but impaired broken-down vestiges of humanity. But when we say that Jesus took on humanity, we are not talking about this kind of humanity. For the humanity of Jesus was not the humanity of sinful human beings, but the humanity possessed by Adam and Eve from their creation and before their fall. ... He was not merely as human as we are, he was more human than we are. He was, spiritually, the type of humanity that we will possess when we are glorified. ...

The incarnation involved a bridging of the metaphysical, moral, and spiritual gap between God and man. The bridging of this gap depended upon the unity of deity and humanity within Jesus Christ. If the redemption accomplished on the cross is to avail for mankind, it must be the work of the human Jesus. But if it is to have the infinite value necessary to atone for the sins of all human beings, then it must be the work of the divine Christ. ...

Having concluded that Jesus was fully divine and fully human, we still face the issue of the relationship between these two natures in the one person of Jesus. This is one of the most difficult of all theological problems. [Erickson, 723-724, 736-737]

Jesus united perfect humanity with perfect deity in a single person. During His time on earth before His crucifixion, He did not yet have His glorified resurrection body, so He would get hungry, thirsty, and weary; He felt pain, and ultimately He would experience physical death on the cross. This was necessary in order for Him to pay the price for the sins of the whole world. But the humanity of Jesus was perfect sinless humanity, which is what humanity was intended to be before sin and the Fall entered the world. Jesus embodied complete deity at the same time. This is how Jesus could be the image of the invisible God. Jesus is the visual aid which we need in order to see and understand what God is like.

The Greatness of Christ as Creator of the Universe

Col 1:15b – the firstborn of all creation,

In the last part of verse 15 Christ is identified as the firstborn of all creation. This same Jesus, the God-Man, who has made the invisible God visible to us, is now described in His relationship to the created universe.

Firstborn is the Greek word *prōtotokos* which means "first to come forth." It can indicate either "priority in time or supremacy in rank." It is typically translated as "firstborn" and depending on the context it can relate to physical birth order (Matt 1:25; Luke 2:7). But the context governs the meaning, and here the context indicates that he is preeminent over all created things. This idea can be traced back to Psalm 89:27, where God declared, "I also shall make him my firstborn, the highest of the kings of the earth." This pictures the Messiah in His role as the coming Davidic King and calls Him the firstborn, indicating His authority over all other kings.

In relationship to the created universe, then, this tells us that Christ is above or over all that has been created. He has authority and supremacy over everything, so this could be translated "He is preeminent over all creation."

Some have tried to use this verse to support the idea that Christ was a created being. But if Paul had wanted to say that, he would have used the Greek word *prōtoktisis* meaning "first-created." Instead he gives Christ first place by saying that He is preeminent over all creation. We know that this is the correct idea because in the very next verse Paul tells us that Christ is the Creator, so logically He Himself cannot be part of creation.

This reminds me of what Jesus said to the apostle John, which is recorded at the end of the book of Revelation: "I am the Alpha and the Omega, the first and the last, the beginning and the end" (Rev 22:13). Or as the apostle Paul wrote in his letter to the Roman church: "For from Him and through Him and to Him are all things. To Him be the glory forever. Amen" (Rom 11:36).

Col 1:17 – He is before all things, and in Him all things hold together.

To end this section about Christ's relationship to all creation, Paul says that Christ is before all things. He is saying that, from the perspective of creation's timeline, God the Son, Jesus Christ, existed with the other members of the Trinity from eternity past. He is before all things. As it says in John 1:1, "In the beginning was the Word, and the Word was with God, and the Word was God."

Paul concludes by saying that all things **hold together** (*sunistēmi*) in Him. Christ is literally sustaining and holding the entire universe together. He not only created it, but He maintains its stable state. If He stopped doing this, the entire creation would completely fall apart or revert to nothingness. One Bible commentator writes: "Christ is not only the one through whom all things came to be, but also the one by whom they continue to exist." [ZNBC] So in this section we have seen the greatness of Christ as Creator and Sustainer of the universe.

The Greatness of Christ as Head over the Church

Col 1:18 – He is also head of the body, the church; and He is the beginning, the firstborn from the dead, so that He Himself will come to have first place in everything.

Since Christ Jesus is before all things and preeminent over all things, then we would logically expect that this idea would also apply to the Church. Here in verse 18 when Paul mentions the Church, he uses the analogy of a physical body. This is a word picture that Paul had developed previously in his letter to the Corinthian church and then afterward to the church in Rome. His main point in those letters for using this analogy was that the individual members of the Church are each indispensable and work together as a unit, so they should use their God-given gifts and abilities to care for one another (1Cor 12:25). Since Paul is writing this letter to the Colossians several years later, we can see that he expects them to know and understand this previous word picture. As we mentioned in the last chapter, the Colossians had been taught well about the basic truths of the faith, and this must also have included the things that Paul and others had already written to the churches throughout the region.

The new information Paul provides here is that if the Church is viewed as a body, then Christ would be the head. This fits perfectly with the context, since Christ is pictured as supreme or preeminent over everything in the universe. **Head** is the Greek word *kephalē* and can mean the actual physical head of a body, as well as figuratively meaning the top or "superior chief, the one to whom others are subordinate." Although this is a clever play on words, the context here points to the figurative meaning, that Christ is the master or Lord over the Church. In his letter to the Ephesian church which was written at the same time as Colossians, Paul expressed it this way: "And He put all things in subjection under His feet, and gave Him as head over all things to the church" (Eph 1:22). So here in Colossians Paul is also emphasizing Christ's headship or rulership over the Church.

Paul then says, "He is the beginning." The Greek word for **beginning** is *archē* which means "the beginning or origin; describing the person or thing that starts or leads something." So in what sense is Christ the beginning of the Church? Paul answers this in the following phrase: "He is the firstborn from the dead." **Firstborn** is again the Greek word *prōtotokos* and in this verse it describes Christ's relationship to the resurrection from the dead. So in this context it is clear that it means "the first to come forth" because Jesus was the first person to experience the kind of resurrection which includes a glorified body. How does this relate to the Church?

The church could not have begun until after Christ's resurrection and ascension, followed by His sending the Holy Spirit to the gathered disciples (Acts 2:4). After His resurrection but before His ascension Jesus gathered the disciples and "He commanded them not to leave Jerusalem, but to wait for what the Father had promised, 'Which,' He said, 'you heard of from Me; for John baptized with water, but you will be baptized with the Holy Spirit not many days from now'" (Acts 1:4-5). It was necessary for Jesus to go away so that He could send the Holy Spirit to the gathered believers (John 16:7). Later Paul wrote to the Corinthian church, "For by one Spirit we were all baptized into one body," (1 Cor 12:13) and that body is the Church. The Church had its beginning on the Day of Pentecost.

Finally Paul says, **so that He Himself will come to have first place in everything**. Christ is preeminent over the Church which He began and sustains, just like He is preeminent over all of creation which He originated and sustains. In the following verses we will see why Christ has the right to headship over the Church.

The Greatness of Christ as Savior of the World

Col 1:19 – For it was the Father's good pleasure for all the fullness to dwell in Him,

Paul begins by summarizing the important facts about Christ. It was the Father's **good pleasure** (*eudokeō*) for all the fullness to dwell in Him. In other words, it seemed good or it was considered to be right and proper, for all the fullness to dwell in Christ. **Fullness** is the Greek word *plērōma*, and it's the second time we've seen this idea so far in this letter to the Colossians. Since Christ is preeminent over everything, here Paul explains this by attributing fullness or completeness to Him. One Bible commentator described it this way:

> The fullness denotes the sum total of the divine powers and attributes. In Christ dwelt all the fullness of God as deity. ... Thus the phrase gathers into a grand climax the previous statements – image of God, first-born of all creation, Creator, the eternally preexistent one, the Head of the Church, the victor over death, first in all things. [Vincent]

Apparently the secular philosophers had used the word **fullness** (*plērōma*) to express the sum total of the supernatural powers and attributes that they believed were divided among various members of the spirit world. But, "Paul counters that false teaching by stating that all the fullness of deity is not spread out in small doses to a group of spirits, but fully dwells in Christ alone." [MacArthur, 52]

To **dwell** is the Greek word *katoikeō* which means "to house permanently." The *plērōma* or fullness of deity in Christ was not a partial or transient thing – it didn't come and go. In Christ the fullness of divine powers and attributes was a permanent aspect of His nature. Beware if someone tries to persuade you that Christ's deity was not a permanent part of His nature. There is absolutely nothing lacking in Christ or His abilities to work on our behalf. As one Bible scholar has said, "There is nothing necessary to be done in our salvation which He is not qualified to do." [Barnes] As we saw in verse 15, Paul reminds us again here that Jesus is the God-Man who is able to accomplish our salvation as described in the following verses.

Col 1:20 – and through Him to reconcile all things to Himself, having made peace through the blood of His cross; through Him, I say, whether things on earth or things in heaven.

To **reconcile** is the Greek word *apokatallassō* which is yet another powerful word describing what Christ accomplished on our behalf. Paul's normal word for **reconcile** is *katallassō* which is an intensified form of the word *allassō* that means "to change or exchange one thing for another." *katallassō* was typically used of two people coming together after a time of hostility, so it carried the idea of changing the state of those who are hostile to a state of peace. But in this verse Paul goes even further by using a double compound word: *apokatallassō*. The preposition *apo* on the front of the word has the meaning "back" and implies a restoration to a previous state from which one of the parties had fallen away. It also includes the idea of the completeness of the reconciliation. One scholar translated it, "to accomplish a thorough change back." That is the kind of reconciliation which Christ accomplished.

So the question is, "Why do we need reconciliation?" The answer goes back to the disobedience of our first parents, Adam and Eve. When they sinned not only were their own lives affected, but their sin was inherited and imputed to the entire race of humanity. As one commentator put it, by their declaration of independence from God they "declared war on God, but God did not declare war on them." [Wiersbe, 118] As the old saying goes, "If God seems distant, who moved?" So how can sinful humanity ever be reconciled to a holy God? God's holiness cannot allow Him to lower His standards, but creatures who are sinful by nature cannot offer God anything that will appease Him. We could never fix our relationship to God, so God took the initiative to fix the relationship. The penalty that God had patiently explained to Adam before they sinned in the Garden of Eden (Gen 2:16-17), must still be paid in full. But God is the only one who has the power to reconcile all things to Himself as this verse states.

How did Christ do it? Here we see that He made peace through the blood of His cross. The death penalty still had to be satisfied. As one theologian has said:

> Sin requires death for its payment. God does not die. So the Savior must be human in order to be able to die. But the death of an ordinary man would not pay for sin eternally, so the Savior must also be God. We must have a God-man Savior, and we do in our Lord. [Ryrie-T, 281]

The Lord Jesus Christ, the God-Man, was the only one who could have reconciled us to God. Twice in this verse Paul used the phrase "through Him" to emphasize that Christ is the channel or conduit through which we receive reconciliation and peace with God.

Paul says that He reconciled all things to Himself, whether things on earth or things in heaven. This statement may give the impression that something is not right with the universe of created things on earth or in heaven, and while it is true that the Fall of mankind did affect creation (Rom 8:22), we also know from the rest of Scripture that it is only human beings who require reconciliation with God (2 Cor 5:18-20). So this phrase gives us a picture of the completeness of the reconciliation that Christ accomplished.

Here in verse 20 we see Christ's selfless act on the cross which procured our reconciliation to God. Now in verse 21 Paul will tell us more about why we so desperately need this reconciliation. He begins by getting very personal with the believers at Colossae.

Col 1:21 – And although you were formerly alienated and hostile in mind, engaged in evil deeds,

The first two words of verse 21 are literally, "And you." So here Paul rather pointedly shifts the focus of attention directly onto the Colossians. The spotlight had been on Christ so far in this section, but Paul abruptly swings it around to shine on the Colossians – as well as on each of us. Formerly, before they put their faith in Christ, they were typical of all of us. Each of us was alienated from God, and it was a deliberate estrangement on our part. The Greek word **alienated** is *apallotrioō* and the tense indicates something that took place in the past with ongoing or continuing effect – we were in a continuing state of alienation from God.

But the news gets worse. Each of us was hostile in mind. **Hostile** is the Greek word *echthros* which means "hostile, or hating and opposing God." The word **mind** (*dianoia*) denotes our "deep thoughts; our ability to think and understand." Our mindset was actively contrary to God and hating His standards and authority.

Finally, not only was our standing and our thinking set against God, but these expressed themselves in our outward actions. We engaged in evil deeds. One commentator expressed it this way: "The alienation of the mind showed itself by wicked works, and those works were the public evidence of the alienation." [Barnes] This is a very grim description of the status of unbelieving humanity. Even a Bible commentator writing in 1887 said,

> That is a severe indictment, a plain, rough, and as it is thought nowadays, a far too harsh description of human nature. Our forefathers no doubt were tempted to paint the "depravity of human nature" in very black colors, but I am very sure that we are tempted just in the opposite direction. It sounds too harsh and rude to press home the old-fashioned truth on cultured, respectable ladies and gentlemen. The charge is not that of conscious, active hostility, but of practical want of affection, as manifested by habitual disobedience or inattention to God's wishes, and by indifference and separation from Him in heart and mind. [Expositors, Alexander Maclaren, 1887]

If someone from the late 1880s could make such a comment, I can only imagine how offended people would be today, well over a century later, at such a negative description of the state of humanity. But this is the truth of God's Word concerning our condition apart from the reconciliation that Christ provides.

Col 1:22 – yet He has now reconciled you in His fleshly body through death, in order to present you before Him holy and blameless and beyond reproach

This verse forms a sharp contrast to the previous verse. It literally begins with "But now." We could translate this as "But now, because of verse 20, because Christ reconciled us by His death on the cross…" The spotlight is now back on Christ and what He accomplished for us.

Here Paul amplifies what he had said in verse 20. He has now reconciled you in His fleshly body through death. We know the facts about the crucifixion of Christ from reading the first four books of the New Testament. In verse 20 Paul had expressed Jesus' death with the words "the blood of His cross," which is his way of saying that Jesus physically died on that cross. Here in verse 22 Paul is more specific so that there will be no confusion about what happened. First of all, Jesus had a fleshly body – he was fully human, although without sin. One Bible commentator has said, "His death could only take place in a body like ours, of flesh." [JFB]

Paul then makes it clear that Jesus did in fact die. The Greek word for **death** is *thanatos* which means "the separation of the soul and the body by which the life on earth is ended." [Thayer] The death penalty was actually paid in full by Jesus when He died.

Next, again in contrast to what Paul had said in verse 21 about the abysmal condition of unsaved humanity, the reconciliation provided by Christ's death now allows Him to present you before God. The Greek word for **present** (*paristēmi*) means to "place beside or to bring close." And the word **before** is the Greek word *katenōpion* which means "in the presence of or directly in front of something." It would have been impossible, apart from the reconciliation that Christ accomplished on our behalf, for a sinful person to come into the presence of a holy God. But now Christ made this possible.

Paul now uses three important words to describe a believer's new position because of his reconciliation to God. **Holy** is the Greek word *hagios* which means "consecrated or separated unto God." **Blameless** is the word *amōmos* which means "without blemish or fault." Finally, **beyond reproach** is the Greek word *anegklētos* which means "that which cannot be called into account, unreproveable, or unaccused." [Thayer] It is a legal term which means that no judicial accusation can be brought against a person. These three things are available to anyone who puts their faith in Christ's work on our behalf.

In the final verse of this section we see that it starts with a conditional clause – there is a condition for gaining all of the benefits that Paul had just listed. By way of background, one theologian has this to say about our reconciliation:

> God's provision of reconciliation is universal. Because of the death of Christ the position of the world was changed – people were now able to be saved. But that alone saves no one, for the ministry of reconciliation must be faithfully discharged by proclaiming the Gospel message. When an individual believes, then he receives the reconciliation God provided in Christ's death (2 Cor 5:18-21). The world has been reconciled, but people need to be reconciled. Universal reconciliation changes the position of the world from an unsavable condition to a savable one. Individual reconciliation through faith actually brings that reconciliation in the individual's life and changes the position of the individual from unsaved to saved. [Ryrie-T, 338]

Col 1:23 – if indeed you continue in the faith firmly established and steadfast, and not moved away from the hope of the gospel that you have heard, which was proclaimed in all creation under heaven, and of which I, Paul, was made a minister.

Verse 23 begins with, **If indeed you continue in the faith**. In English we have only one kind of conditional clause: "If you do this, then you receive the result." But in the Greek language there were several types or classes of conditional sentences, and here we have what is called a first class conditional clause which is often called a "condition of fact." First class conditional sentences are saying that if something is true, and we assume for the sake of the argument that it is true, then the result will occur. This type of conditional clause puts the most positive spin on the sentence. Sometimes it can be translated by saying, "Since you are continuing in the faith." So Paul certainly does put their continued faithfulness in a positive light.

Continue is the Greek verb *epimenō* which is an intensified form of the word "to continue or persevere." One language expert said that the preposition "*epi* adds to the force of the linear action of the present tense (continue and then some)." [RWP] The tense of the verb indicates a present continuous action, so we might translate this "If you keep on continuing on in your faith."

Paul then gives three descriptive terms that explain how they can accomplish this. First, he says **firmly established** which is the Greek word *themelioō*. This was a term from architecture or construction which pictured laying a firm foundation for a building. It means to remain well-grounded or unwavering on the base of their faith in and knowledge of God. The perfect tense indicates the completed state of the foundation – there is nothing more or different that they require. **Steadfast** is the word *hedraios* which means firmly seated and unmovable. **Not moved away** uses the word *metakineō* which means "not moved away and placed somewhere else." So they are to "keep on continuing on in faith" by standing firm in the hope of the gospel they have heard.

We saw earlier how they heard the gospel message from Epaphras and that they had already been well taught in the truths of the faith. Here Paul is saying, "Stay put. Stick to the truth. You need nothing more than what you already have."

Paul's final point in this section will help him to transition into the next section of his letter to the Colossians, and it has to do with the gospel message. He says this gospel is being proclaimed in all creation under heaven. Previously in verse 6 Paul had said the gospel was bearing fruit in all the world. Both there and here Paul may be using hyperbole to express how widely the message was being disseminated across the known world of his day. One Bible scholar has said, "The message has been heralded abroad over the Roman Empire in a wider fashion than most people imagine." [RWP]

Then Paul states his final point: **I, Paul, have been made a minister of this gospel message to the world.** This is where we will pick up our study of this letter to the Colossians in the next chapter.

We have covered a lot of ground in this chapter, and that means that there will probably be many things for which we can give thanks to God in our prayers.

– Let's check our ideas about Jesus. Do we have an accurate image of Him as fully human in the best possible way as well as being fully God?

– One thing that should help us view Jesus as fully God is His role in the creation of the universe. Not only did He create everything, but He is actively holding it all together even now.

– Christ is greater than every created authority, either in heaven or on earth. He needs nothing else – there is nothing He lacks – because He has permanently embodied all the fullness of deity as part of His nature.

– It was Christ's great plan and purpose that the Church Age would occur and that He would be the beginning and head of the Church. He led the way and provided our hope of following Him in His resurrection from the dead with a glorified body.

– One of the richest truths is that Jesus provided a way for us to be reconciled to God when there was no other way. He voluntarily took the death penalty which each of us rightly deserved.

– Now Christ can bring us into the presence of a holy God because He has made us holy and blameless and beyond reproach.

– As we rely on the indwelling strength of God, let us keep on continuing on in our faith, standing firm and unmovable on the basic truths which we have learned.

Paul's Passion for the Church

(Colossians 1:24-2:5)

In the last chapter we saw that Paul ended by urging the Colossians to continue on in the faith, which he identified as "the gospel that you have heard, which was proclaimed in all creation under heaven, and of which I, Paul, was made a minister" (Col 1:23). Recall that in the very first part of this passage we saw how Paul was made a minister when Christ Himself appeared to Paul on his way to Damascus to persecute believers there. Jesus confronted Paul and caused him to see the truth about all that He had accomplished, and then Jesus commissioned Paul as His special representative or apostle to the Gentiles (see Acts chapters 9, 13, 22, and 26).

After his encounter with Jesus on the way to Damascus, Paul spent the next 30 years of his life carrying out his God-given mission to spread the gospel. He traveled widely, from the Holy Land and the Middle East, to the Roman provinces throughout Asia Minor, Greece, Macedonia, and Italy – some even speculate that his journeys throughout the Mediterranean took him as far as Spain. In the very first chapter of this book we saw Paul himself tell about all of the things that he had already suffered for the sake of the churches during his ministry.

Once when Paul and Silas were unjustly imprisoned in the Macedonian city of Philippi, we see how he handled that time of suffering and mistreatment. Acts 16:23-25 says,

> When they had struck them with many blows, they threw them into prison, commanding the jailer to guard them securely; and he, having received such a command, threw them into the inner

prison and fastened their feet in the stocks. But about midnight Paul and Silas were praying and singing hymns of praise to God, and the prisoners were listening to them.

This is typical of how Paul rejoiced during his sufferings. So as this next section of Paul's letter to the Colossians begins, Paul says:

Col 1:24 – Now I rejoice in my sufferings for your sake, and in my flesh I do my share on behalf of His body, which is the church, in filling up what is lacking in Christ's afflictions.

When Paul is writing this letter he is under house arrest and awaiting trial in Rome. So even in the midst of imprisonment, Paul is rejoicing since he knows that he is not suffering because he committed a crime against society, such as theft or murder. The last eight chapters of the book of Acts explain why Paul was now being held under house arrest in Rome. The only reason for his imprisonment is because he was faithfully fulfilling his mission to proclaim the gospel.

The word translated **sufferings** is the Greek word *pathēma* which means "mistreatment or hardship." And Paul adds that his sufferings have been for your sake. His mistreatment has been in the line of duty – he has been working on their behalf to benefit them, but he's had to deal with mistreatment and opposition to his ministry almost everywhere he has gone. As Jesus told His disciples in John 15:19, "If you were of the world, the world would love its own; but because you are not of the world, but I chose you out of the world, because of this the world hates you."

The next set of phrases in this verse are accurately translated into English, but in the original Greek the word order is different. The only reason I mention this is because the phrases "I do my share" and then later "in filling up" are actually a single word in Greek, but the English translation separates the ideas from each other. The Greek word *antanaplēroō* is a very rare double compound word from *plēroō* (to fill) which means "to fill up in turn." Paul is saying that it is now his turn – or as it's translated here, I do my share. He is filling up or carrying forward what Jesus said would happen – to Himself as well as to those who are His, which we previously mentioned in John 15:18-20.

Paul says it is his turn to experience the opposition and pressure that Jesus promised would come to His followers, and he expresses it this way: in filling up what is lacking in Christ's afflictions. First we need to understand what he means by Christ's afflictions so that we can determine what is lacking.

The word **afflictions** (*thlipsis*) means "pressure or trouble." It is never used in Scripture to describe the suffering of Christ on the cross. Earlier in this letter Paul had clearly taught that nothing whatsoever was lacking in Christ's accomplishment through His death on the cross. Christ's work on the cross was complete and sufficient for redeeming all mankind and reconciling the world to God. So here, Paul cannot be saying that there is something lacking in Christ's death on the cross. But there were other pressures and troubles that Christ experienced during His earthly ministry. One Bible commentator has said:

> The word afflictions is never used in connection with the death of our Lord; so it must apply to His pre-cross suffering caused by the pressure of Satan and human adversaries, not to speak of the apathy and unbelief of the people. It is appointed to all believers to have a share in this kind of suffering (Acts 14:22; Phil 1:29; 2 Tim 2:3). [Harrison, 42]

The word **lacking** is the Greek term *husterēma* which means "what follows behind or is yet lacking." One Bible scholar called them the "left-over" afflictions. Again, this takes us back to Jesus' final words to His disciples in the upper room: "These things I have spoken to you, so that in Me you may have peace. In the world you have tribulation [the same Greek word, *thlipsis*], but take courage; I have overcome the world." (John 16:33)

Paul says that his sufferings are "in my flesh." We have already looked at some of the things which Paul endured during his ministry, and the phrase "in my flesh" reminds me of what Paul wrote to the Galatian church when he said, "From now on let no one cause trouble for me, for I bear on my body the brand-marks of Jesus" (Gal 6:17). Paul's many mistreatments must have resulted in fleshly scars that were very much in evidence all over his body, and he considered these to be his Lord's badges of ownership in his flesh.

Paul made it clear that he was not doing this for his own benefit or for his own glory. He said he endured everything "on behalf of Christ's body, which is the church." This is yet another way Paul could say that he was filling up what is left of Christ's afflictions. The Church is Christ's body, so Jesus experiences anything that happens to the members of His body. As Jesus said to Paul while on his way to Damascus to continue persecuting the Church, "Saul, Saul, why are you persecuting Me?" (Acts 9:4; 22:7; 26:14). To afflict the Church is to afflict Christ, too.

There may yet be some of these remaining afflictions which you and I might be called upon to endure for the sake of Christ and His Church.

Col 1:25 – Of this church I was made a minister according to the stewardship from God bestowed on me for your benefit, so that I might fully carry out the preaching of the word of God,

In this verse Paul elaborates on what he had said in verse 23, that he had been made a minister of the gospel. Here he says that his appointed role was according to the stewardship from God. The word **stewardship** is not one that we use very often today. It is from the Greek word *oikonomia* which is sometimes translated "economy, administration, or the method of operating something." It carries the idea of the obligation, responsibility, and authority to manage things. Paul was given a special stewardship over the Church – it was ultimately (as he says here) "for your benefit." Literally, it was focused toward or into the Church, for establishing it and building it up in the faith.

The final phrase literally says, "to complete the word of God." The words **fully carry out** are translating the Greek word *plēroō* which we have seen several times before and which means "to fill to the top so that nothing is lacking for a full measure; to fill to the brim; to make complete in every way." It is accurately translated here as "to fully carry out the preaching of the Word of God," even though the word "preaching" was inserted by the translators in order to express the thought. This was the apostle Paul's primary mission. He was faithfully proclaiming the message of Christ's work on our behalf. But there was something beyond even that task which Jesus was using Paul to accomplish, and we will see what that extra something was in the very next verse.

Col 1:26 – that is, the mystery which has been hidden from the past ages and generations, but has now been manifested to His saints,

In this verse we see that there was information which God had kept hidden from past generations, but He was now making this information publicly known to His saints through the apostle Paul. So Christ is using Paul as a channel of new revelation for the New Testament Church. Jesus used Paul literally to "complete" the Word of God for the Church.

The term he used here to express this idea is the Greek word **mystery** (*mustērion*). This is the first time we have seen this word in Paul's letter to the Colossians, but it is one that he used previously in his letters to the Thessalonians, Corinthians, Romans, and Ephesians. Because Paul had taught this concept previously, he would expect the Colossians to understand what he means by it. Here he provides a brief definition of the term by saying that a mystery is something "which has been hidden from the past ages and generations, but has now been manifested to His saints." In other words, a **mystery** is new revelation – a truth that was hidden or unrevealed in the Old Testament. As it says in Deut 29:29, "The secret things belong to the Lord our God, but the things revealed belong to us and to our sons forever." God kept some of His plans secret until the proper time for them to be revealed. One Bible scholar expressed it this way:

> Mystery refers to the secret thoughts, plans, and dispensations of God that are hidden from humanity and can only be known through divine revelation. ... By the time Paul was writing, the mysteries had been well revealed to the apostles and New Testament prophets and, for that reason, they were to lay down the foundation of the church (Eph 2:19-22), and they were to record New Testament revelation (Eph 3:1-10). It can now be understood by the saints with the help of the indwelling Holy Spirit (1 Cor 2:14). [DPT, 274]

The basic Greek word *mustērion* means a secret, and the ancient so-called "mystery religions" carefully guarded their unique secrets. This knowledge was only to be shared among the initiates, and they were promised salvation through their secret ceremonies and rituals. A vow of silence restricted the adherents from sharing any information with those outside. Many of these mystery religions were actively practiced in the known world of Paul's day, and some people in the Colossian church may have been rescued – to use Paul's words – out of that dominion of darkness.

But the New Testament definition of **mystery** was quite different. It is simply a truth that was previously unrevealed by God but which He has now shared by revealing it to His apostles and prophets. There are no esoteric truths, no vow of silence, no secrecy in practicing arcane rituals. The revealed truth is publicly available to all, just as God offers salvation to all through the reconciling work of Christ on the cross. This was now part of the apostle Paul's mission or stewardship for the Church – to clearly share any new aspects of God's will and plan that were revealed for the Church Age.

Col 1:27 – to whom God willed to make known what is the riches of the glory of this mystery among the Gentiles, which is Christ in you, the hope of glory.

We saw in the last verse that the mystery has been manifested to His saints. **Manifested** was the Greek word *phaneroō* which means to bring something to light and to make it clear. Here in verse 27 he says that "God willed to make known this mystery." The word **willed** means that God had intended, planned, or determined to do this at exactly the right time.

To **make known** (*gnōrizō*) carries the idea of declaring or revealing something in order to make it fully known. But notice that Paul does not say that God merely "makes known this mystery." Instead he says that God "made known the riches of the glory of this mystery." This mystery is glorious and full of richness. **Riches** is the Greek word *ploutos* which means "wealth, abundance, plenty." And **glory** is the Greek word *doxa* which means "resulting in praise and honor to God." Paul used a similar expression when he wrote to the Ephesians around the same time as this letter to the Colossians. He said, "that you will know what is the hope of His calling, what are the riches of the glory of His inheritance in the saints" (Eph 1:18). All of the things we have in Christ bring us a glorious abundance beyond what we could ever ask or imagine.

Before Paul tells us what this mystery is, he first explains that it is being offered to the Gentiles. As one Bible commentator has said, "This is the crowning wonder to Paul that God had included the Gentiles in his redemptive grace, and that Paul himself has been made the minister of this grace among the Gentiles (Eph 3:1-2). He feels the high honor keenly and meets the responsibility humbly." [RWP]

The new truth which God is revealing to us through the apostle Paul is expressed in just a few simple words in this verse. Paul writes: "Christ in you, the hope of glory." As one Bible scholar explained:

> The Gentiles are in focus, as this mystery involves them. ... The fact that the Messiah now indwells every believer is the mystery unrevealed in the Old Testament. ... While the Old Testament revealed many things about the coming Messiah, His Person, His message, and His program, it never revealed that He would indwell every believer. This is now revealed in the New Testament, fulfilling the promise that Jesus made in John 14:20 (I am in you). [Fructenbaum, 682]

This is a profound truth which is expressed so simply here. God, by His Spirit in each believer, has taken up permanent residence in them. As it says in Eph 2:22, "You are being built together into a dwelling of God in the Spirit." Christ dwells within us by His Spirit. Here Paul calls this the hope of glory. As Paul was writing one of his last letters to his right-hand man Timothy, he said, "Christ Jesus, who is our hope" (1 Tim 1:1). If all we have is Jesus, we have all we need both for today and for the glorious future.

Col 1:28 – We proclaim Him, admonishing every man and teaching every man with all wisdom, so that we may present every man complete in Christ.

As Paul continues to write about the ministry to which Jesus appointed him, he explains how he carries out his mission, as well as what his ultimate goal is for all the believers whose lives he touches. How does Paul communicate the message about Christ?

First, he **proclaims** Him. This is the Greek word *kataggellō* which means to announce (*aggellō*) throughout (*kata*) or "to proclaim far and wide." This is Paul's ministry of publicly declaring or making known the truths about Christ and what He accomplished to reconcile the world to God.

Next, he **admonishes** every man. This is the Greek word *noutheteō* which means "to put in mind;" to warn or admonish someone gently. First people need to know the facts about the work of Christ on our behalf, and then they need to understand the consequences for failing to accept and act on those facts.

Then, he **teaches** every man. This is the Greek word *didaskō* which means "to instruct or deliver information." This is where the truths of the faith or the content of biblical doctrine are carefully presented to every believer. This is the job description for every pastor during the Church Age in which we are living today.

Paul says he does this with all wisdom, meaning that he teaches in a practical way which helps the learner to understand and apply the teaching to their lives. In addition, one commentator has said, "This is opposed to the idea of esoteric wisdom (represented by the mystery religions) with higher knowledge given only to a select few. In Christian teaching the highest wisdom is freely open to all." [Vincent]

Finally, Paul gives his ultimate goal for this work. "So that we may present every man complete in Christ." Here Paul uses the same word he used in verse 22 when he said that Christ "has now reconciled you in His fleshly body through death, in order to present you before Him holy and blameless and beyond reproach." The Greek word *paristēmi* means to "place beside or to bring close." I think that Paul has in mind that scene he mentioned previously, where Christ is presenting us to the Father.

And Paul wants to do everything he possibly can to make sure that every believer is complete in Christ. The word **complete** is the Greek word *teleios* which carries the idea of something having reached its final goal or its full expression of maturity. Some have expressed Paul's goal as producing "spiritual adults in Christ, no longer babes in Christ, mature and ripened Christians, fully-grown in Christ." This is the condition of the Colossians that Paul was praying for earlier in Col 1:9-12. He wants them to grow in spiritual maturity through the teaching ministry which he and others have been given for the Church.

Notice that three times Paul repeated the phrase "every man" in order to emphasize that every individual without exception is offered the reconciliation that Christ procured by His death on the cross. Christianity is not some obscure mystery religion or secret cult into which only a few are allowed membership.

Col 1:29 – For this purpose also I labor, striving according to His power, which mightily works within me.

Here Paul explains what energizes him as he labors and strives. The Greek word for **labor** is *kopiaō* which means "to grow weary from toil or exhausted with wearisome effort." It can express exhaustion from carrying burdens or experiencing grief. **Striving** is the Greek word *agōnizomai* which sounds very much like our English word "agonizing." It means "to contend with adversaries; to struggle with difficulties and dangers."

But here we also see that Paul was not laboring and striving in his own strength, expending his own meager resources. Instead Paul worked using "His power which mightily works within me." In chapter 1 verse 11 Paul had prayed for the Colossians that they would be "strengthened with all power" using the Greek word *dunamis*, from which our English word dynamite comes. We saw that verse could literally be translated "powered with all power." Here we again see (literally) "His power which powerfully works within me." *Dunamis* is used in both places, and the Greek word **works** is *energeō* from which we get our English word "energy." Paul is presenting himself as the "poster child" for living in the strength that God provides.

Col 2:1 – For I want you to know how great a struggle I have on your behalf and for those who are at Laodicea, and for all those who have not personally seen my face,

In the previous section Paul expressed his desire for every individual believer to grow into spiritual maturity, and starting in this verse he expresses his desire for the entire fellowship of believers in Colossae. Paul wants them to know that, even though they live in a small market town which has no apparent claim to the attention of the leaders of the Church, they are known and seen. They are of concern to others and they do matter to the Church at large.

Paul uses a form of the same word he used in 1:29 when he says he wants them to know "how great a struggle he has on their behalf." **Struggle** is the Greek word *agōn* which means "an inward contest of anxiety" for the church at Colossae. He was literally agonizing over them. And not only for them, but for the believers in Laodicea and the whole Lycus Valley. These were people to whom Paul had not personally ministered, as it says here – "those who have not personally seen my face." But Paul's concern would be like the love and care that a grandfather might have for his grandchildren. Paul was their spiritual grandfather, since they were one "generation" removed from him spiritually. He is concerned that his lineage would continue on a firm foundation of the truths of the faith.

Col 2:2 – that their hearts may be encouraged, having been knit together in love, and attaining to all the wealth that comes from the full assurance of understanding, resulting in a true knowledge of God's mystery, that is, Christ Himself,

He goes on to express his desire for the entire group of believers in that area. He wants their hearts to be **encouraged** which is the Greek word *parakaleō*. It means "to call alongside to help" and it is a form of the same word Jesus used to describe the ministry of the Holy Spirit in John 14:16. Paul says in the next phrase that one of the most encouraging things about the Colossian fellowship of believers is that their hearts are **knit together** in love. This expresses the Greek word *sumbibazō* which means "to push together or unite in affection." As he says later in Col 3:14, unconditional, selfless, sacrificial love is the glue that binds them all together. And we know from Col 1:4 that the Colossians were already demonstrating this type of love for all the saints.

Paul also desires that they experience all the wealth that comes from understanding the truths of the faith. This is the same word he had used in Col 1:27 when he talked of the *riches* of the mystery. Here again he uses the Greek word *ploutos* which means "wealth, abundance, or plenty." There is a sense of being the richest man in town when the believer truly understands what he has been given in Christ.

This sense of abundance results from **full assurance**, which is the Greek word *plērophoria*. It means "perfect certainty or complete conviction." This one word by itself probably would have been sufficient to get his idea across, but Paul goes on to say "full assurance of understanding," which is the same word he used already in Col 1:9 when he said that he had "not ceased to pray for you and to ask that you may be filled with the knowledge of His will in all spiritual wisdom and understanding." One other thing that Paul had prayed in 1:9 is also amplified here in this verse when Paul adds, "resulting in a true knowledge of God's mystery." **True knowledge** is a proper English translation for the Greek word *epignōsis* which we also saw previously in Col 1:9. It means "thoroughly understanding, recognizing the importance, accepting and applying something personally in our lives."

At the end of this verse Paul restates the mystery he previously revealed in Col 1:27 – that is, **Christ**. In Col 1:27 he briefly described the mystery as "Christ in you" – the Messiah indwelling the believer. Here Paul abbreviates it even more using a single word – Christ.

Col 2:3 – in whom are hidden all the treasures of wisdom and knowledge.

If people in Paul's day were craving some kind of hidden or secret knowledge, as some of the Greek mystery religions were doing, then Paul gives believers the win by saying in effect, "If you have Christ then you have all the treasures of **wisdom** (*sophia*) and **knowledge** (*gnōsis*) that anyone could ever desire." The word **treasures** is the Greek word *thēsauros* which looks and sounds like our English word "thesaurus." It means "the place in which precious things are laid up and valuables are kept." Christ is our treasury because in Him we have all of the riches and wealth and abundance that we could even need.

Col 2:4 – I say this so that no one will delude you with persuasive argument.

Paul had already commended the Colossians for their faithfulness to the word of truth, the gospel. It was constantly bearing fruit and increasing as they were growing in their knowledge of Christ toward full spiritual maturity. But here Paul warns them that there may come a time when others might try to deceive them with persuasive arguments intended to derail them from the true way they had come to believe and follow.

Delude is the Greek word *paralogizomai* which means "to deceive by false reasoning." The world of Paul's day was awash with traveling orators and philosophers. As one commentator has said, this refers to "artful words, smooth and plausible arguments, such as were employed by the Greek sophists and rhetoricians." [Barnes]

Persuasive argument is a single Greek word, *pithanologia* which means "persuasiveness of speech, specious discourse which leads listeners into error."

One Bible scholar described them as the "enticing words and false reasonings of those who seek to take advantage of believers and turn them away from the simplicity of the gospel. Both their manner and their matter are suspect. ... Paul is suggesting that teaching contrary to the faith owes more to the skill and subtlety of its advocates than to any supposed truth in the words that are presented." [Harrison, 51] Paul will spend more time discussing this issue in the upcoming sections, but here we see the first hint that trouble may be on the horizon for the Colossians.

Col 2:5 – For even though I am absent in body, nevertheless I am with you in spirit, rejoicing to see your good discipline and the stability of your faith in Christ.

In the final verse of this section we see Paul reassuring the Colossians that even though he is not physically present with them, he is with them in spirit – doing everything he can to encourage them, warn them, and build them up in the faith. And here Paul also takes the time to commend the Colossians for two important things.

First, he rejoices to see their good discipline. **Good discipline** is the single Greek word *taxis* which is a military term. It means an orderly arrangement, and carries the idea of proper order or a well-regulated life. Paul commends them for the positive and orderly way in which they are conducting their lives and their church activities. One commentator has said, "Their order encourages him to think that they will not be swept off their feet by persuasive talk or be inclined to depart from the guidance which the present letter affords." [Harrison, 52]

Next, Paul commends the stability of their faith in Christ. **Stability** is the Greek word *stereōma* which is also a military term that means "strong, solid, or stable." He is saying that the Colossians are well established in their faith, their knowledge, and their trust in Christ. This is a wonderful affirmation of the strength and stability of the believers in Colossae. In the next chapter we will hear more about Paul's warnings to the Colossians regarding possible threats to their faith.

One application we can take from this section is to ask ourselves how we are dealing with the trials and pressures we experience in life. Are we grumbling and complaining, or are we rejoicing in God's sovereign care over us? Are there any afflictions which you are being called upon to endure for the sake of Christ and His Church?

Next, how is your intake of the preaching of the Word of God? Are you exposing yourself to a regular dose of solid expository preaching? Are you in a church or fellowship which regularly teaches the truths of God's Word and the doctrines of the faith? If not, then what steps do you want to take in order to place yourself within reach of the sound teaching of the Bible?

Are you part of a local fellowship of believers that allows your heart to be encouraged? Are you being knit together in love with fellow Christians? Someone has wisely said that,

> Loving someone is not defined by having warm feelings toward them, but by meeting their needs. The last time you made a sacrifice for someone was the last time you loved him or her. Love is first action, then the emotions follow. So the strengthened heart is a heart that has learned to love. [MacArthur, 89]

How can you put this kind of love into action this week?

Finally, let us all practice good discipline and struggle to maintain the stability of our faith in Christ this week. There are so many influences all around us that distract us and can derail us in our focus on Christ.

Let's be aware of things that might sound good to our ears, but which really have the goal of steering us subtly off the narrow path of devotion to Christ.

Walk in the Riches of Christ

(Colossians 2:6-15)

As we have seen in the previous chapters, what Christ has accomplished on our behalf brings us glorious riches (Col 1:27). We have all the wealth that comes from the treasure of wisdom and knowledge in Christ. And as the advertising pitchmen on commercials sometimes say, "But wait! There's more!"

Seriously, though, there really IS more to the riches we have in Christ, and Paul is going to describe some of these additional things in today's passage. He begins by saying ...

Col 2:6 - Therefore as you have received Christ Jesus the Lord, so walk in Him,

Therefore is a key word which usually indicates a transition in the flow of thought, and this is the first time we have seen this word so far in the book of Colossians. We could translate it this way: "In view of everything that has been said before." Someone once said, "When you see the word therefore, look back to see what it's there for." If we want to understand why Paul used the word "therefore" here in Colossians 2:6, we should look back to the immediate context to see what he has been building up to in his flow of thought.

As we review what Paul has said so far in this letter, one thing we notice is that the subjects of the sentences have changed periodically. We could chart them this way.

Section	Sentence Subject	Topic
Col 1:1 - 14	First person	thanks and prayer
Col 1:15 - 23	Third person	greatness of Christ
Col 1:24 - 2:5	First person	Church ministry
Col 2:6 - 23	Second person	admonitions

In general the primary subjects of the sentences for the first fourteen verses in chapter one are in the first person. Paul tends to use **I** or **we** when he is talking about himself, his appreciation for the Colossians, and his prayer for them. However, in the next section – verses 15 through 23 – when Paul is talking about the greatness of Christ, he tends to use the third person in referring to the wonderful things which **He** (Christ) accomplished on our behalf.

In the passage we covered in the last chapter – Colossians chapter 1 verse 24 through chapter 2 verse 5 – Paul switched back to using the first person (**I** or **we**) when he talked about his ministry on behalf of the Church. So as we look over the section we will be covering in this chapter, there is a definite change in the subject of the sentences. In general Paul will now begin using the second person ("**you**") as he discusses how the work of Christ applies directly to the Colossians.

The first time we saw Paul use the second person (you) was in chapter 1 verse 21 when he put the spotlight briefly on the Colossians to illuminate their lost and hopeless condition before they put their faith in Christ. But as we begin this new section in chapter 2, Paul is making a major transition or shift in subject.

He says, "as you have received Christ Jesus the Lord." The word **received** is the Greek word *paralambanō* which literally means "to receive near." Paul is using this word the same way he used this same word **learned** in Col 1:7 – where he said they had learned the word of truth, the gospel, from Epaphras when the church in Colossae was originally established.

Paul does not use the phrase "Christ Jesus the Lord" in any of his other letters. So here we can take this phrase to mean that the Colossians received, accepted, and believed three important truths about Christ. First, Jesus is the **Christ** or Messiah which God promised in the Old Testament. This emphasizes that Jesus is the Savior of the world. Second, the Messiah or Christ is identified as the human person whose name was **Jesus**. This emphasizes the complete humanity of Jesus, which was necessary in order for Him to pay the death penalty for the sins of mankind. Third, Jesus is the **Lord** – this is the Greek word *kurios* which refers to His sovereignty and supreme authority. This is the title that is given to God the Messiah. So in this brief description Paul sums up all that he has already taught about the deity, humanity, and supremacy of Jesus.

He finishes this verse by commanding them to "walk in Him." He is saying, "As a result of everything you have learned so far about Christ Jesus, put these truths into action in your life and your lifestyle." **Walk** is the Greek word *peripateō* which we already saw in chapter 1 verse 10, where Paul prayed that as they continue to grow in spiritual maturity they would "walk in a manner worthy of the Lord, to please Him in all respects, bearing fruit in every good work and increasing in the knowledge of God." In that verse Paul prayed that this might be true of the Colossians, but here in this verse Paul is commanding them to do it. The verb is a present imperative – "continually do this" or "keep on doing this." He wants them to demonstrate the impact Christ has had on them by habitually living in a way that glorifies Christ.

Col 2:7 - having been firmly rooted and now being built up in Him and established in your faith, just as you were instructed, and overflowing with gratitude.

In this verse Paul is elaborating on how this will look to those around the believers who are watching them. He combines several different word pictures in order to communicate his point. First he pictures a tree which has deep roots that hold it firmly in place. He says "having been firmly rooted." **Rooted** is the Greek word *rhizoō* which means "to strengthen with roots; to be firmly grounded." The perfect tense indicates something that happened once in the past, but which is having continuing results in the present. This seems to picture the time of their original planting as seedlings when they first heard the truths of God's Word, followed by their continued growth toward maturity in Christ.

Next he says, "being **built up** in Him." The Greek word *epoikodomeō* means "to build upon" so here Paul pictures the construction of a building level by level on a solid foundation. One Bible scholar expressed it this way: "As rooted implies their vitality, so built up implies massive solidity." [JFB]

The present tense indicates something that is continually in process, just as the spiritual growth of the Colossians is a continuing process over time. This is coupled with the word "**established**" which is the Greek term *bebaioō* that means "to make firm or stable." Both words are in the present tense, indicating that each level of the building being constructed is stabilized before the next phase is added.

These word pictures remind us of what Paul said in chapter 1 verse 23: "If indeed you continue in the faith firmly established and steadfast." The Colossians can accomplish this if they will allow themselves to be built up in their faith, especially through the ministry of those whom God has sent to them in the church. Here Paul adds, "just as you were **instructed**" which is the Greek word *didaskō*. It's the same word he used in chapter 1 verse 28 where he said that it was his job to "teach every man." The teaching ministry of the Church is the primary means through which believers are able to grow toward spiritual maturity as they are built up and established in the truths of the faith.

Finally, Paul says that they should be "overflowing with gratitude." This was also one of the steps toward spiritual maturity that Paul prayed for the Colossians in chapter 1 verses 9-12. He said, "so that you will walk in a manner worthy of the Lord, to please Him in all respects, bearing fruit in every good work and increasing in the knowledge of God; ... giving thanks to the Father, who has qualified us to share in the inheritance of the saints in Light." But here in chapter 2 verse 7 Paul tells them what the extent of their thankfulness should be. Here he says, "**overflowing** with gratitude" and he used the Greek word *perisseuō* which means "to superabound; to furnish so richly so that there is an overflowing abundance." One Bible commentator said this means: "Expressing overflowing thanks to God since you have been made acquainted with truths so precious and glorious. If there is anything for which we ought to be thankful, it is for the knowledge of the great truths respecting our Lord and Savior." [Barnes]

Col 2:8 - See to it that no one takes you captive through philosophy and empty deception, according to the tradition of men, according to the elementary principles of the world, rather than according to Christ.

We saw in the last chapter how Paul included a brief warning to the Colossians in chapter 2 verse 4 when he said, "I say this so that no one will delude you with persuasive argument." Here in this verse Paul will expand on what he meant by that warning. He starts by saying, **See to it** which is the Greek word *blepō* – "to be on the lookout or to be watchful and aware of any signs of danger." This is an imperative or command in the present tense, which indicates that they are to be constantly on the lookout.

What does Paul want them to watch out for? He describes a danger here, followed by a list of the means by which the Colossians might fall into that danger. The way Paul expresses it is "that no one **takes you captive**." The danger is described using the Greek word *sulagōgeō* which literally means "to carry off as a captive or slave" or "to be led away and made subject to one's captor." Paul then lists the means by which a believer might be vulnerable to this danger.

First, he says, "through philosophy." Some say that the Greek term **philosophy** (*philosophia*) was coined by Pythagoras in the 6th century BC when someone called him wise. He insisted that he was not wise but merely a seeker with a deep affinity for exploring human wisdom. Around 530 BC he is said to have traveled to southern Italy where he established a school in which his disciples were sworn to secrecy and lived a communal, ascetic lifestyle. He attempted to provide rational explanations for the world as a whole, and his contributions covered a wide range of topics, including mathematics, astronomy, music, mysticism, prophetic visions, and speculations about the immortality of the soul.

Pythagoras was an example of one of the early philosophers, but after him came Socrates, Plato, Aristotle, and so many more that they are difficult to keep track of. The early philosophical systems or schools included Cynicism, Epicureanism, Hedonism, Idealism, Materialism, Skepticism, and Stoicism among many others. In the ancient world of Paul's day there was a centuries-old tradition of philosophy that permeated the culture and society. One commentator says:

> Greek philosophy was common in the regions around Colossae and they were exposed to the influences of these plausible systems. Philosophy included speculations about the nature of the divine existence, and the danger to the Colossians was that they would rely on the deductions of that fallacious reasoning, rather than on what they had been taught by their Christian teachers. [Barnes]

So this is the kind of danger that Paul warns the Colossians about, both in chapter 2 verse 4 as well as here in verse eight.

Second, Paul says, "and empty deception." **Empty** is the Greek word *kenos* which means "resulting in nothing; having no effect; destitute of spiritual wealth." It was used to describe someone who would boast of his faith but do nothing to demonstrate any of the fruits of faith. **Deception** is the Greek word *apatē* which means "deceitfulness." It seems that Paul is making a play on words here, because the philosophers' highest goal was what they called virtue, which is the Greek word *aretē*. So here Paul is saying that what they called *aretē* (virtue) is actually *apatē* (deception).

The content of those philosophies was based on speculative but plausible-sounding explanations. However, their ideas were not rooted and established on the truth of divine revelation as were the doctrines they were being taught by their church leaders. One commentator explains what Paul is saying in these words:

> It would be going beyond the evidence of our text to assert that Paul is lashing out at all philosophy as worthless or even dangerous. The kind he has in mind is clear from the further description of it as "vain deceit," a system which has no substance and no power to edify. Those who hold it are self-deceived. Why, then, should genuine believers in Christ leave the solid reality of the faith for a spiritual vacuum? [Harrison, 56]

Paul describes this philosophy as being "according to the tradition of men." **Tradition** simply means something that is given over or passed on between people. The context must determine the meaning. As one Bible scholar commented,

> "The word is colorless in itself. The tradition may be good (2Th 2:15; 3:6) or bad (Mk 7:3). Here it is worthless and harmful, merely the foolish theories of the philosophers." [RWP]

There is such a thing as Christian tradition, and prior to the New Testament the gospel and the truths for the Church Age were communicated by the authoritative teaching of the apostles which were shared among the believers. But the same thing was true of the dangerous traditions of the philosophers. Paul is calling for the believers to exercise discernment in following the truths of divine revelation while rejecting the empty theories of the philosophers.

Paul also describes those philosophies as being "according to the elementary principles of the world." The phrase **elementary principles** is a translation of the single Greek word *stoicheia*, and the basic meaning is "any orderly arrangement or series of elements." This simplistic term was used in various ways to describe quite different things. Some of the possible uses include:

- the letters of the alphabet as the elements of speech
- the elements from which all things in the universe are made
- the rudiments or fundamental principles of any art or science
- the heavenly bodies as parts of the solar system
- the spirits or spiritual forces which influence the world

It is important to let the context determine the meaning which Paul intended here. It seems that there are two possible ways we could translate this word in this verse.

First, Paul may be saying that those philosophical ideas are simplistic and limited to only what humanity might speculate upon using finite and flawed human perception and reasoning. One commentary explained it this way:

> These words are characteristic of St. Paul, who was profoundly conscious of the supernatural origin of his own doctrine (see Gal 1:11-17; 1Co 11:23; 1Th 4:15: comp. John 3:31-35; John 8:23; 1Jn 4:5). "The rudiments of the world" are the crude beginnings of truth, the childishly faulty and imperfect religious conceptions and ideas to which the world had attained apart from divine revelation (comp. Gal 4:3, Gal 4:9; also Heb 5:12, for this use of *stoicheia*). [Pulpit]

A second option might be that Paul is referring to the supposed hierarchy of spirit beings that were included in some of the ancient philosophies of the day. One commentator expressed it like this:

> Many ancient mystery religions thought of the world as a dangerous place, threatened by spirits or spiritual forces they called elements or elemental forces. They thought one was protected from these dangerous spiritual forces by either worshiping them or by finding a greater deity or spiritual power that was superior to these elements. [Guzik]

This second option gains some support from Paul's description of the so-called rulers and authorities that were created by Christ (Col 1:16) and over whom Christ is the head (Col 2:10). Then in Col 2:15 Paul will tell us that He "disarmed the rulers and authorities, made a public display of them, having triumphed over them through Christ." One commentator said,

> There is considerable debate among scholars as to this phrase. It is applied to the spirits which are thought of as controlling the forces of nature. Since the veneration of angels is referred to in Colossians 2:18 and since in verse 8 the stoicheia are contrasted with Christ, the possibility of a reference to spirit beings should be admitted. [Harrison, 57]

These two options explain why some English Bible translations have different renderings. For example:

– "elementary principles of the world" = NASB, NKJV, CSB
– "elemental spirits of the world" = ESV, NIV, NLT, NET, RSV

So finally, here in Colossians 2:8 Paul ends this verse by saying, "rather than according to Christ." He spent the bulk of his time describing the danger which he wanted to warn the Colossians about, but now at the end of the verse he introduces the antidote or countermeasure for all of these things. As one scholar said, "Christ is the yardstick by which to measure philosophy and all of human knowledge. The philosophers were measuring Christ by their philosophy as many men are doing today. They have it backwards. Christ is the measure for all human knowledge since he is the Creator and the Sustainer of the universe." [RWP]

As we saw in verse 3, all the treasures of wisdom and knowledge are hidden in Him, so there is no point in seeking something more or better than what we have in Christ. Any claim by worldly wise men to have discovered something better is nothing more than empty deception. As we paraphrased what Paul said in chapter 1 verse 23, "Stick to the truth. You need nothing more than what you already have."

Christ and His work to reconcile humanity to God have effectively nullified and superseded any so-called worldly wisdom. And now that Paul has started talking about Christ again, he goes on to refresh our memory concerning the truths about Christ shared so far in this letter.

Col 2:9 - For in Him all the fullness of Deity dwells in bodily form,

In chapter 1 verse 19 Paul already told us that "it was the Father's good pleasure for all the fullness to dwell in Him." Here in this verse, though, Paul is even more specific. The word **for** could be translated **because** – it presents the reason for saying at the end of the last verse that Christ supersedes every worldly system of wisdom. So Paul says "In Christ all the fullness of deity dwells bodily." Here there can be absolutely no doubt about what the fullness consists of. Not only is Christ fully God, but He is also fully human. This may be the clearest statement in all of the Bible about the person of Christ.

One theologian had this to say about the errors and heresies associated with the person of Christ:

> Someone has said that there are only seven basic jokes, and every joke is merely a variation on one of them. A similar statement can be made about heresies regarding the person of Christ. There are basically six, and all of them appeared within the first four Christian centuries. They either deny the genuineness

(Ebionism) or the completeness (Arianism) of Jesus' deity, deny the genuineness (Docetism) or the completeness (Apollinarianism) of his humanity, divide his person (Nestorianism), or confuse his natures (Eutychianism). All departures from the orthodox doctrine of the person of Christ are simply variations on one of these heresies. [Erickson, 738]

So, since the fullness of deity permanently dwells in Christ, Paul goes on to say ...

Col 2:10 - and in Him you have been made complete, and He is the head over all rule and authority;

The original Greek sentence structure is important for understanding this thought. It is not that we have been made complete – but that He was made complete, and as long as we are **in Him** then we can partake of the completeness that is His. It could be translated literally as "You are in Him who has been made complete."

The word **complete** is *plēroō*, which is the verb form of the noun used in the previous verse to express that the fullness of deity dwells in Christ bodily. *plēroō* means "to fill to the top so that nothing is lacking." This is not the same word that Paul had used in chapter 1 verse 28 where he said, "so that we may present every man complete in Christ." There he used the word *teleios*, which would be better translated as "mature" in that verse since it means "fully developed or having reached its goal." It can be confusing when different underlying Greek words are translated using the same English word. In Col 1:28 it means "mature" but here in Col 2:10 it means "filled with His fullness."

In the second part of this verse Paul says that He is the head over all rule and authority. In chapter 1 verse 16 we saw that Christ created all rulers and authorities, whether earthly or heavenly. So here in this verse we see that, just as Christ is supreme over all created things, here He is specifically identified as the head over all rule and authority. The context in this section makes it clear that when Paul speaks of rule and authority, he is talking about spirit beings in the heavenly realm. In verse eight he had mentioned the elemental spirits (*stoicheia*) who have a role in deceiving believers and leading them astray. This will gain further support later in verse 15 when Paul describes how Christ defeated the rulers and authorities.

Col 2:11 - and in Him you were also circumcised with a circumcision made without hands, in the removal of the body of the flesh by the circumcision of Christ;

In this verse Paul mentions **circumcision** which is the Greek word *peritemnō*, meaning "to cut around." This term can be used in one of two ways based on the context:

First, it can mean the literal surgery of cutting around the foreskin. The following references explain why this rite was not required of Christians (Acts 15:5; 1 Cor 7:19; Gal 2:3; 5:2; 6:12-13).

Second, it can be used metaphorically to mean "the removal of the sins of the flesh." This is how it is used in the following New Testament passages (Rom 2:29; Phil 3:3), and this usage is also seen throughout the Old Testament (Deut 10:16; 30:6; Jer 4:4).

It is clear that the second metaphorical meaning is what Paul intends here in Col 2:11, because the type of circumcision he refers to is "made without hands." So Paul is not referring to some Jewish teachers who were trying to convince the Colossians to submit to the rite of circumcision. Paul had already dealt with that issue many years earlier in his letter to the Galatian believers who were facing that exact issue. One Bible scholar has said:

> Since this is without hands, the flesh is not corporeal here; rather it refers to the sinful nature of man. ... Since the text goes right on to speak of burial with Christ, the circumcision of Christ must refer to the value of His death for all those who are mem-

bers of His body. [Harrison, 60]

So the circumcision Paul mentions here has to do with the sin nature which every person was born with after the Fall of Adam and Eve. The fullness we have in Christ is able to give us the desire and power to control the impulses of our fleshly nature. Later in this letter Paul will deal specifically with some of these fleshly impulses which believers are to control.

Paul now goes on to mention the rite of baptism, which is practiced by Christians as a sign of our identification in the death, burial, and resurrection of Christ.

Col 2:12 - having been buried with Him in baptism, in which you were also raised up with Him through faith in the working of God, who raised Him from the dead.

In this verse Paul very briefly describes the significance of the rite of baptism, with its symbolism of being buried with Christ and then raised up with Him. He is not talking about the physical act of being immersed in water, but is referring to the spiritual identification believers have with the death, burial, and resurrection of Christ which gives us the power to control the sins of the flesh. Paul explains that the rite of baptism (like the rite of circumcision) does not have any saving power in itself. As he says here, it is "through faith in the working of God" that believers experience Christ's fullness applied to their lives. As one commentator said, "Lest any get the impression that the rite itself is able to effect this life change, the apostle is careful to add that, in submission to the rite, the candidate is expressing his faith in the God who raised His Son from the dead." [Harrison, 61]

Col 2:13 - When you were dead in your transgressions and the uncircumcision of your flesh, He made you alive together with Him, having forgiven us all our transgressions,

Previously in chapter 1 verse 21 we saw that Paul began the sentence with the words "And you." In Col 1:21 he said, "And you once having been alienated and hostile in mind in evil deeds." Here in chapter 2 verse 13 he does the same thing when he literally says, "**And you** being dead in trespasses and the uncircumcision of your flesh."

We can see that Paul is elaborating on the truths which he presented previously in this letter. Before our faith in Christ, we were alienated, hating God's claim on us, and engaged in selfish, evil deeds. In chapter 2 verse 13 Paul continues to describe that wretched state when he says we engaged in transgressions against God arising from our sin nature, which results in eternal separation from God through death. In chapter 1 verse 22 Christ's solution was to die in our place in order to reconcile us to God. There Christ's death solved the problem of our own death sentence. In chapter 2 verse 13 the emphasis is on the new life which God gives us in Christ.

In chapter 1 verse 14 Paul had told us that Christ provided **forgiveness** of sins, but there he used a different Greek word, *aphesis* which means "sending away" to provide freedom or release. Here in chapter 2 verse 13 Paul uses the word *charizomai* which means "unmerited pardon." It is a gracious gift given to us by God through faith in the working of God.

Col 2:14 - having canceled out the certificate of debt consisting of decrees against us, which was hostile to us; and He has taken it out of the way, having nailed it to the cross.

Not only has God forgiven all our transgressions, but there was something else that existed which provided irrefutable evidence of our guilt before a holy God. There was a **certificate of debt**, which is the Greek word *cheirographon*. Chirography simply means handwriting, but it was commonly used to mean a certificate of debt or a bond agreement which was written or signed by someone in order to make it legal.

But what was this set of decrees which put us under a debt that we could never pay?

It was the moral law of God, which applies to the Gentiles as much as to the Jews. It represented God's perfect standard of holiness, which fallen humanity could never reach. And it was against us as well as hostile to us. As one commentator has said,

> It is against us, because it comes like a taskmaster, bidding us comply, but neither putting the inclination into our hearts nor the power into our hands. And it is against us, because the revelation of unfulfilled duty accuses the defaulter and reveals his guilt. And it is against us, because it comes with threats of penalty and pain. It stands as both accuser and avenger against us. [Maclaren in Vincent]

So how did God solve this problem for us?

First, He has **canceled** it or wiped it away. The Greek term *exaleiphō* means to completely obliterate, erase, or sponge away. Plato used it of blotting out writing, which was the practice of rubbing or scraping a parchment so that it could be reused.

Second, He has t**aken it away**. This is the Greek word *airō* which means "to take upon one's self and carry what has been lifted up." This same word was used by John the Baptist when he looked toward Jesus and said, "Behold the Lamb of God who takes away the sin of the world" (John 1:29). The perfect tense emphasizes that the certificate of debt has been permanently removed, has been paid or canceled, and cannot be presented again.

Third, He has nailed the certificate of debt to the cross where it was paid in full by the substitutionary death of Christ. One commentator explained it this way:

> It is said that there is an allusion here to the ancient method by which a bond or obligation was canceled, by driving a nail through it, and affixing it to a post. ... If this be the meaning, then the expression here denotes that the obligation ceased on

the death of Jesus, as if he had taken them and nailed them to his own cross, in the manner in which a bond was canceled. [Barnes]

All of these things were accomplished by Christ on the cross. Add to this what Paul previously explained in chapter 1 verse 14 where he said that Christ **redeemed** us. And in chapter 1 verse 20 he told us that Christ **reconciled** us to God, "having made peace through the blood of His cross." So many important things happened on that cross, and in the last verse of this section Paul will mention one more thing that Christ accomplished there.

Col 2:15 - When He had disarmed the rulers and authorities, He made a public display of them, having triumphed over them through Him.

Here Paul says that God disarmed the rulers and authorities. We know that those same rulers and authorities were originally created by Christ (Col 1:16), and Paul also stated that Christ is head over all ruler and authority (Col 2:10). So the context of this section helps us to understand that when Paul writes about the rulers and authorities, he is talking about spirit beings which are arrayed against God and anyone who belongs to Him. This may lend support to the idea that the Greek word *stoicheia* should be translated as "elemental spirits" in Col 2:8.

The word **disarmed** is the Greek word *apekduomai*. This is a rare double compound word that Paul used twice and only in his letter to the Colossians. It is from the two words *apoduō* and *ekduō*. Paul simply combines the two in order to express how completely the rulers and authorities have been stripped of their power or disarmed.

Paul goes on to say that God did not do this secretly, but instead he made a **public display** of their defeat. This comes from the word *deigmatizō* which means "to openly make an example of something." God celebrated His triumph over them or led the vanquished foes in a triumphal procession because of what Christ accomplished on the cross. The writer of the book of Hebrews explained how Christ's death on the cross stripped Satan and his demons of their power when he said, "Therefore, since the children share in flesh and blood, He Himself likewise also partook of the same, that through death He might render powerless him who had the power of death, that is, the devil, and might free those who through fear of death were subject to slavery all their lives." (Heb 2:14-15)

Since Christ Jesus the Lord has done all of these things for us, why would we pursue any other so-called wisdom or knowledge? We literally have more than we could ever ask or hope in Christ alone.

As we look at our walk or our lifestyle, given all of the riches we have in Christ, are there some areas which need attention? Are we living in a way that would please Him? Which area needs the most attention?

– Being built up in your faith through solid Bible teaching,
– Expressing gratitude to God,
– Avoiding the sins of the flesh.

Are there worldly ideas which you may have been taught and have accepted as true, but which are really just empty speculation? What things do we believe which may be contrary to the truth of God's Word? If you have specific things which fall into this category, you can begin by looking for Bible verses which counteract the empty philosophies of the world.

Do you have any thoughts or desires that you are yielding to but which come from your fleshly nature? Paul will have more to say about these things in the upcoming sections, but for now if you see something in your life that you aren't sure would please God, bring that area to Him in prayer and ask for wisdom for dealing with it.

Are there things in your life which you are having a difficult time forgiving yourself for? Take this opportunity to remember that Christ has forgiven you, and He has nailed those things to the cross. If the God of the universe has forgiven you, don't you think it's time to try forgiving yourself?

Wrong Ways to Master the Flesh

(Colossians 2:16-23)

In this chapter we will cover the last part of Colossians chapter 2, which forms an important transition between what the apostle Paul has said in the first part of this letter and what he will tell them in the upcoming section. So far Paul has been quite complimentary to the Colossians as he has commended the steadfastness of their faith in Christ and their love for all the saints.

He has also shared some amazing truths about the greatness of Christ – not only about what Christ has done for us, but truths about Christ's very nature and character. As the Creator, He is head over all things – and all the fullness of deity dwells in Him bodily. All the treasures of wisdom and knowledge are in Christ, and (best of all) the Lord Jesus Christ indwells every believer, providing the desire and power to live in a manner worthy of the Lord to please Him and to bear fruit in every good work.

The overall tone of his letter so far has been positive and encouraging, although twice Paul has given the Colossians a warning to watch out lest they are led astray from the truths of the faith. He begins this section by saying, "**Therefore**…"

This means that what Paul has to say in today's passage is the logical follow-up to what he has just said in the previous passage. He stated in verses 9-10 that, in Christ the fullness of deity dwells bodily, and believers partake of the fullness because they are in Him. Then Paul shared two pictures that help us to understand how we are identified with Christ so we can live in Him.

First in Col 2:11 Paul mentioned "circumcision made without hands, by putting off the body of the flesh, by the circumcision of Christ." When he speaks of "putting off the body of flesh" he is talking about gaining mastery over our fleshly, sinful nature. One commentator expressed it this way: "Of course by flesh here we are to understand, not merely the body, but the whole unregenerate personality, the entire unrenewed self that thinks and feels and wills and desires apart from God." [Expositors]

We know that the rite of circumcision has no spiritual effect in itself, but it is symbolic of how Christ made it possible for us to put off the sins of the flesh which we are prone to by nature.

Then in Col 2:12 Paul said we have been "buried with Him in baptism, in which you were also raised up with Him through faith in the working of God." He went on to say in Col 2:13 that "when you were dead in your transgressions and the uncircumcision of your flesh, He made you alive together with Him." Like the rite of circumcision, the rite of baptism has no spiritual effect in itself, but it is symbolic of our death to sin and our resurrection to new life in Christ. It is a public testimony of our complete identification with Christ who makes it possible for us to put off the sins of the flesh and to put on righteous attitudes and behaviors since Christ Himself is indwelling us and providing the power to overrule our fleshly desires.

So here at the end of Col 2, Paul will discuss three sets of things that are the wrong way to master our fleshly desires. Then starting in Col 3 he will describe the right way to do this, and he will specifically identify what we are to put off, followed by what we are to put on as a result of living our life in Christ and for His glory.

How do we know that verses 16 through 22 have to do with mastering our fleshly nature? The answer is in verse 23 – the last verse in this section – where Paul summarizes what he says in verses 16 through 22. He identifies the three sets of things using these terms:

- self-made religion (Col 2:16-17)
- self-abasement (Col 2:18-19)
- severe treatment of the body (Col 2:20-22)

His conclusion is that these things are "of no value against fleshly indulgence." Paul's summary statement shows us the structure of this section, with the topic being wrong ways to master the sin nature. Paul says, ...

Col 2:16 - Therefore no one is to act as your judge in regard to food or drink or in respect to a festival or a new moon or a Sabbath day--

This set of things involves man-made dietary rules and the observance of specific festival days on the calendar. Those who are promoting these "traditions of men" are implying that following this set of rules will result in greater spirituality.

The verb is a present active imperative in the third person, and what Paul is forbidding here is the habit of someone who is continually passing **judgment** on believers in such matters. The Greek verb *krinō* is probably the most general word for judging and it carries the idea of considering and deciding. It refers to making a simple distinction between one day and another (Rom 14:5).

The set of things that are mentioned here – food, drink, festivals, new moon rituals, and the Sabbath – have often been identified as the Jewish dietary laws and national feast days which God mandated in the Mosaic Law. If they are meant to indicate Jewish traditions, then they are probably referring to the additional rules and regulations which the elders created as a so-called "fence around the Law." They consist of restrictions which go beyond what is revealed in God's Word, and they can legitimately be described as "self-made religion." This is what Jesus condemned in the Pharisees when He said, "Rightly did Isaiah prophesy of you hypocrites, as it is written: 'This people honors Me with their lips, but their heart is far away from Me. But in vain do they worship Me, teaching as doctrines the precepts of men.' Neglecting the commandment of God, you hold to the tradition of men." (Mark 7:6-13)

Except for the mention of the Sabbath, however, these terms are general enough that they could also refer to some of the known rules and celebrations in the pagan mystery religions. So what Paul says could apply equally well to those dietary restrictions and festival days. His point is that believers are not to be held to a legalistic set of rules in order to measure their spirituality or to maintain their relationship with Christ. The reason is given in the very next verse.

Col 2:17 - things which are a mere shadow of what is to come; but the substance belongs to Christ.

All of the things mentioned in verse 16 are mere shadows of the reality which believers have in Christ now and more of which they will experience with Christ in the future. This is very similar to the wording of Heb 10:1, which says, "For the Law, since it has only a shadow of the good things to come and not the very form of things, can never, by the same sacrifices which they offer continually year by year, make perfect those who draw near."

The rules and regulations were a shadowy reminder that the reality is in Christ. Our life in Christ is not maintained or measured by behavioral checklists. It is a living, vital connection to our Lord and Savior through the enabling power of the indwelling Holy Spirit. One commentator expressed it this way: "Why should one grasp for a shadow when he holds the substance in his hand?" [Harrison, 66]

So, obeying dietary restrictions and observing ritual festival days will have no benefit in helping you to keep or enhance the true spirituality you already have in Christ.

Col 2:18 - Let no one keep defrauding you of your prize by delighting in self-abasement and the worship of the angels, taking his stand on visions he has seen, inflated without cause by his fleshly mind,

Now, the second set of things is in the category which Paul called self-abasement, both here in verse 18 and in his summary in verse 23. Like the phrase "act as your judge" in verse 16, here the verb is also a present active imperative in the third person, so Paul is forbidding the action of someone who is continually declaring believers ineligible for their rightful prize. The Greek verb *katabrabeuō* means "to decide against or to declare someone unworthy of his prize." This word is parallel to "judging" in verse 16, but it is an even stronger or more forceful expression.

The Greek phrase that is translated "delighting in self-abasement" is somewhat difficult and obscure, but probably the best way to state it in this context would be "having the appearance of great modesty, or false humility." This kind of demeanor was apparently one of the main characteristics of those who were promoting this set of behaviors. As one commentator expressed it, "The persons referred to took pleasure in entering into the hidden and esoteric things of religion. They desired to appear to do this with a humble spirit." [Barnes] So the term self-abasement describes the approach or demeanor of those who were advocating these things.

The two main items included in this set are 1) the worship of angels, and 2) ecstatic visions. The Greek word **worship** (*thrēskeia*) applies to any external religious ritual or ceremonial observance. Specifically here, what is being advocated is a ceremony involving angels, or possibly angelic mediators between God and man. This is something that the Jews would never participate in, so it definitely eliminates them as the ones who were advocating this set of activities. There were, however, many other groups in Paul's day that did revere the so-called "elemental spirits." Several different Greek mystery religions included doctrines and rituals having to do with appeasing the spirit world. Even today, astrology and occult practices abound.

Part of the uncertainty about translating and interpreting this verse may be because Paul was using the exact wording that was common to some of the advocates of mysticism in his day. As one Bible scholar has said,

> The obscurities, which make it one of the hardest passages in the entire book to decipher, may be due in part to Paul's desire to show that he is familiar with what is being promoted at Colosse, which he does by crowding the text with terms that would be meaningful to his readers but which are obscure to us. It may be, too, that he is using language ... designed to show up the whole cult as ridiculous and thereby shame his readers into the realization of the folly of being taken in by it. [Harrison, 66-67]

The second thing mentioned is that someone is "taking his stand on visions he has seen." The phrase **taking his stand** is a translation of the single Greek word *embateuō* which has several different meanings. It can mean "to enter into or come into possession" of something; or it can mean "to investigate or go into the details" of something; or it can mean "to enter frequently." One Bible scholar lists several ancient inscriptions where the word is used "of an initiate in the mystery cults who 'set foot in' (*enebateusen*) and performed the initiation rites. Paul is here quoting the very work used by these initiates who 'take their stand on' these imagined revelations in the mysteries." [RWP]

It is a purely private and subjective thing to have visions or claim to see mystical things that no one else can see. As one commentator said, "The vision is a mark of the esoteric character of the religion." [Harrison, 68] Unfortunately there is no way to verify the validity or the truth of what is being experienced or described by such a person. And, far from being humble, such a person is actually "inflated without cause by his fleshly mind." One commentator states, "Paul minces no words in showing how, contrary to supposed self-abasement, this person really is puffed up without reason by his sensuous mind." [Harrison, 68] The claim to having ecstatic visions would have been a powerful statement that attracted peoples' attention, if not their devotion, in the culture of Paul's day. He then goes on to explain why this set of issues is so dangerous to the Church.

Col 2:19 - and not holding fast to the head, from whom the entire body, being supplied and held together by the joints and ligaments, grows with a growth which is from God.

Up to this point in Paul's letter to the Colossians he has not given any clear indication that the dangers he warned against had actually crept into the churches of the Lycus Valley. But here in verse 19 we do see a sign that the person claiming spiritual visions is "not holding fast to the head, from whom the entire body, being supplied and held together by the joints and ligaments, grows with a growth which is from God."

To be accused of not holding fast to the head would imply that the person was part of the body, the Church, and that he should be vitally connected to the head, who is Christ. As Paul stated in Col 1:18, Christ is the head of the body, and it is from Him that the entire body is supplied and held together so that it can grow in a healthy manner. So there may have been a church attender in Colossae who was advocating ecstatic visions as a way to become closer to God and to enhance one's spirituality. As we will see later, ecstatic experiences were a common practice in the region of Phrygia.

But false humility, the worship of angels, and ecstatic visions have no benefit for enhancing the link that you already have to Christ. In fact, Paul states that these things indicate you have severed your link to Christ – you have lost touch with the head. He says that such a person is inflated without cause by his fleshly mind.

Inflated is the Greek word *phusioō* which comes from the word for a bellows. It can mean to puff up something, or to be inflated with pride and arrogance. So, the appearance of humility or self-abasement is actually a cover for pride, arrogance, and a superior attitude.

It is the fleshly mind that is the source for these things. A literal translation is, "by the mind of his flesh." The human mind plus the sin nature is a dangerous combination. Together they can devise all sorts of ungodly things. What believers must rely on is the mind guided by the indwelling Spirit and the truths of God's Word. Apart from the Spirit and the Word, the fleshly mind is quite unreliable – even for a believer. In the next chapter of this letter Paul will have much more to say about the right way to master the sin nature by means of a godly mindset.

Col 2:20-21 - If you have died with Christ to the elementary principles of the world, why, as if you were living in the world, do you submit yourself to decrees, such as, "Do not handle, do not taste, do not touch!"

The third set of things have to do with severe treatment of the body or what we might call asceticism. This is expressed by Paul in a single interrogatory sentence – "Why do you submit to man-made decrees?" But, as usual, Paul packs precious truths around this simple question.

He begins by saying, "If you have died with Christ to the elementary principles of the world." As mentioned in a previous chapter, there are several classes of conditional sentences in Greek. Here we have a first class conditional clause which means that we assume for the sake of the argument that the condition is true. With this type of conditional clause we might translate this verse, "**Since** you have died with Christ." This takes us back to the picture of baptism in which a believer identifies himself with the death, burial, and resurrection of Christ (Col 2:12-13). As it says in verse 13, "when you were dead in your transgressions and the uncircumcision of your flesh, He made you alive together with Him." Everything else that Paul says here in verse 20 depends on the believer's death to the world and his new life in Christ. As one commentator expressed it:

> Death with Christ, already considered in verse 12, is now set forth as that which separates one from the rudiments of the world. The redeemed are set free from man-made regulations mistakenly concocted to make one more holy. [Harrison, 69]

So, those who have placed their faith and trust in Christ for their eternal destiny have been freed from any obligation to obey these kinds of man-made decrees. Believers already have everything they could ever need in Christ, so why would they seek something more? Believers already partake of the fullness through Christ, so what more could possibly be gained by following man-made regulations to abstain from certain things? The believer's cup is already full to overflowing, so there is nothing more of value that can possibly be added.

The decrees or rules that were proposed had to do with abstaining from specific things. They were items that could be handled, tasted, and touched. There were many groups in the culture of Paul's day who taught that a person's spirituality or continued relationship with God depended on faithfully keeping outward rituals and avoiding specific consumables. We can use the word "consumables" because that is what Paul calls these things in the next verse.

Col 2:22 - (which all refer to things destined to perish with use)--in accordance with the commandments and teachings of men?

The things that they were being told not to handle, taste, or touch are all things that perish with use. As one commentator expressed it: "They are all destined for corruption, for physical decomposition, in the very act of consumption. You cannot use them without using them up. They are destroyed at the very moment of being used." [Expositors] So, the things that they are being asked to abstain from have no permanent existence and no significance in themselves.

It is an interesting fact that what seem to be polar opposites, asceticism and hedonism, are two sides of the same coin. Asceticism encourages self-denial while hedonism values luxurious indulgence, but they both fall into the same error. As one commentator has said:

> Asceticism and luxury have in common an overestimate of the importance of material things. The one is the other turned inside out. The reveler in his purple and fine linen, and the ascetic in his hair shirt, both make too much of "what they shall put on." The one with his feasts and the other with his fasts both think too much of what they shall eat and drink. A man who lives on high with his Lord puts all these things in their right perspective. [Expositors]

As well as pertaining to things that are perishable, Paul says these decrees or prohibitions are "in accordance with the commandments and teachings of men." As he said earlier in Col 2:8, they are "according to the traditions of men rather than according to Christ." In other words, they lack divine authority. These rules and regulations are not in accordance with God's Word.

Col 2:23 - These are matters which have, to be sure, the appearance of wisdom in self-made religion and self-abasement and severe treatment of the body, but are of no value against fleshly indulgence.

This verse contains Paul's summary statement and it provides the structure for the entire passage. As was mentioned earlier, he identifies three issues using these terms:

– self-made religion (Col 2:16-17)
– self-abasement (Col 2:18-19)
– severe treatment of the body (Col 2:20-22)

Earlier Paul expressed his desire that "no one delude you with persuasive argument" (Col 2:4) and here in verse 23 he acknowledges that some of these matters have the appearance of wisdom. All of the things Paul has mentioned in this section at the end of chapter 2 may look promising from a human perspective, and they can appeal to our fleshly nature. Unfortunately, people find it easier to submit to rigid external rules and regulations, but much more difficult to submit to the inner promptings and working of the Holy Spirit in our lives.

But as we have already mentioned, none of these things provide any power for mastering the sin nature. One commentator expressed it this way:

> The milder forms of putting oneself to pain, hair shirts, scourgings, abstinence from pleasant things with the notion that merit is thereby acquired or sin atoned for, have a deep root in human nature, and hence "a show of wisdom." It is strange that people should think that, somehow or other, they recommend themselves to God by making themselves uncomfortable, but so it is that religion presents itself to many minds mainly as a system of restrictions and injunctions which forbids the agreeable and commands the unpleasant. [Expositors]

Paul's conclusion is that these things are "of no value against fleshly indulgence." So we see that all of the things in today's passage cover the wrong ways to master the flesh. As one scholar said,

> All these ordinances have no power to keep that sinful self down, and therefore they seem to Paul as so much rubbish. Therein lies its conclusive condemnation, for if religious observances do not help a man to subdue his sinful self, what, in the name of com-

mon sense, is the use of them? There is only one thing that will put the collar on the neck of the flesh, and that is the power of the indwelling Christ. [Expositors]

As we come to the end of Colossians chapter 2, Paul has led us to the point where we eagerly desire to know about the right way to master our fleshly desires. So Paul will begin the next chapter by answering our questions about the best way to deal with our sin nature by means of a godly mindset.

Detour: the "Colossian Heresy"

I'd like to take a short detour to discuss an issue that many of you probably have noticed in our study of the book of Colossians.

If you have stayed with me so far in this study, you'll know that I tend to approach the text of the Bible using the traditional grammatical-historical method of interpretation. This means that we study the words and sentences of the text, as well as looking into the historical situation at the time of its writing, to discover the meaning of the text as the original author would have intended and as the original readers would have understood it. This is why I tend to spend quite a bit of time on word studies and sentence structure, as well as determining what an expression would have meant to the readers in the culture and society of that day. Simply put, we are trying to let the Word of God speak for itself.

With the apostle Paul's letters to the different churches, though, this can be a challenging task because what we have in the Scriptures is only half of the conversation. It would be like eavesdropping on someone's telephone call and trying to reconstruct the entire message by listening only to one side of the conversation. There are parts of the conversation that we may need to guess or speculate about in order to make sense of what we are hearing.

In a way, that is what Bible scholars do when interpreting the epistles in the New Testament. They are trying to determine why Paul wrote what he did. What was the situation that caused Paul to word things the way he did? Was there an error that Paul was arguing against, but which he didn't specifically identify by name? These are some of the questions that trustworthy Bible scholars are trying to answer.

In order to accomplish this task, scholars look at all of the issues or symptoms that Paul recorded in the letter, and they try to put those individual puzzle pieces together to form a picture of the situation. In a way, it is like trying to solve a jigsaw puzzle without having the actual photo on the lid of the puzzle box to guide the placement of the pieces.

Like when solving such a puzzle, the tendency is to try fitting all of the pieces into a single overall picture or unified explanation of the situation. This is what reputable Bible scholars have been doing for several centuries. You may have noticed that almost every Study Bible and Commentary on the book of Colossians will have a section in which the author tries to identify what is often called "the Colossian Heresy." They are trying to put all the pieces together to create a single picture.

The assumption is that there was a group of false teachers in the church at Colossae who were promoting a heresy about the nature and work of Christ, as well as making judgments about spirituality based on the kinds of behaviors we've looked at today in this section of Colossians 2.

When Paul writes "don't do this or that," it's logical to assume that there were false teachers in the church who were actively leading believers into those errors. Many assume that when Paul emphasizes a particular doctrine, he is doing so because he knows that doctrine is being neglected by the church. Because Paul spent so much time describing the greatness of Christ and His work, the assumption is that the false teachers' system of theology was minimizing Christ's nature and work, or relegating Christ to a position of one of many other spiritual beings who influence our world.

Let's briefly take a look at the symptoms of the issue that Paul wrote about in his letter to the Colossians. There are some common themes that apply to all of them. They are characterized as empty deception, the traditions of men, and self-made religion. When we lay out the puzzle pieces we can group them into roughly four basic categories: 1) the worship of spirits, 2) asceticism, 3) the observance of special rituals and days, and 4) ecstatic inspirations or visions. One final category that I added is whether or not the error or heresy has historically been known to originate in Phrygia.

On the right side of the chart (page 95) there are examples of some of the philosophical systems or religions that have been proposed by scholars as being part of the "Colossian Heresy." These items are listed based on the approximate time period during which they were known to appear and operate in history.

First on the timeline is historic Judaism, but the only checkbox we can mark for traditional Judaism is the observance of special rites and feasts. As the Jewish Encyclopedia states, "The history of both Judaism and the Jews is, on the whole, free from ascetic aberrations." In a moment we will see two exceptions to this statement, but when searching for a system that constitutes the "Colossian Heresy" we can eliminate historic Judaism from the list.

Second on the timeline is the Greek mystery religions and philosophical systems. We see here that all of the checkboxes are marked under this category. The only reason for this, though, is that there were so many different schools over its long history that examples exist for all of the Colossian symptoms in some of the schools. But no one Greek mystery cult or school of philosophy can account for all of the checkboxes on its own. There was one specific mystery religion that originated in Phrygia, which was the cult of Cybele around 200 BC. This may have had an influence in the tendency toward ecstatic visions, which we briefly mentioned previously. On the whole, though, there is no evidence that a single Greek philosophy or mystery religion is what constituted the so-called "Colossian Heresy."

Third on the timeline is Jewish Mysticism which was practiced from around 100 BC. This is sometimes referred to as "Merkabah Mysticism" from the Hebrew word which means chariot. It was a type of Jewish mysticism which included visions like those in the book of Ezekiel chapter 1 or as described in the *hekhalot* or "palaces" literature. There was a fascination with stories of ascents to the heavenly palaces and viewing the Throne of God, with an emphasis on ecstatic experience. This was an aberration in Jewish thought that was discouraged or prohibited by the rabbis. Since it only added the mystic element to Judaism, it is also not comprehensive enough to account for the "Colossian Heresy."

The "60 AD" line in the chart indicates that this was the approximate time when Paul wrote to the Colossian believers, and we see that the existence of the Essenes does overlap that period. So, fourth on the timeline is Essenism, which was also an outlier in Jewish thought. The history of the Essenes was short-lived, and they are best known for preserving the Dead Sea Scrolls in caves near their desert community. They were a splinter group who took the regulations of the Pharisees beyond their extreme. They practiced asceticism, celibacy, ritual baptism, communal living, strict observance of the Sabbath and holy days, studying and preserving the secrets of the elders, and reverence for angelic beings. Even though the Essenes check many of the boxes, their system did not include all of the symptoms described by Paul, and they were never known to have traveled or lived in the area of Phrygia.

The Search for a Colossian Heresy

Common items:
2:8 - empty deception; traditions of men; self-made religion

Worship of Spirits 2:8 - elemental spirits; 2:15 - hierarchy of rulers and authorities in the spirit realm; 2:18 - false humility and angel worship
Asceticism 2:21 - do not handle/taste/touch; 2:23 - severe treatment of the body
Observance of Special Rituals/Days 2:16 - food or drink; festival, new moon, sabbath
Ecstatic Inspirations 2:18 - visions he has seen
Originated in Phrygia

Fifth on the timeline is Montanism, which did not formally appear on the scene until almost a century after Paul was writing to the Colossians. I list it here because it was known as the "Cataphrygian Heresy" since it originated in Phrygia. Montanus had been a priest in the cult of Cybele, but he joined the church and as a recent convert he claimed to have the gift of prophecy. He manifested ecstatic visions and spoke in unintelligible tongues, similar to what he experienced as a pagan priest. Formal Montanism occurs too late in history and does not check all of the boxes to account for what Paul described, but it does include several of the elements mentioned in Paul's letter to the Colossians, especially the regional tendency to mysticism.

The last item on the timeline is Gnosticism, which did not appear on the scene until over a century after Paul wrote to the Colossians. It is included in the list because most reliable

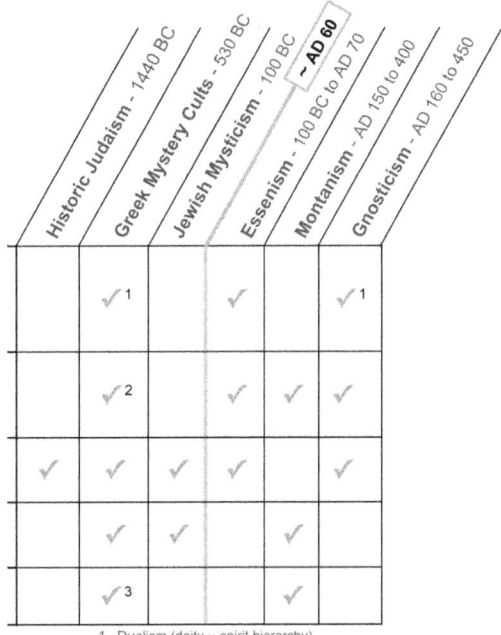

1. Dualism (deity → spirit hierarchy)
2. Pythagorean School & Stoicism (e.g.)
3. Cult of Cybele - 200 BC

Commentaries and Study Bibles discuss Gnosticism as forming at least part of the "Colossian Heresy." Gnosticism fostered exclusiveness by distinguishing an enlightened elite, who were those with special knowledge (*gnōsis*). Their so-called knowledge was often gained through mystical or occult means. They believed that matter was evil, so a holy God could have no contact with the world. They taught that God put forth a series of intermediate spirit beings, each a little more distant from Him, so that at the end of the chain there was one with enough deity to create the world of evil matter, but far enough removed from God so that His purity was not compromised. The Gnostics revered these intermediary spirit beings. And because they believed that matter was evil, they practiced asceticism and the severe treatment of the body. We can see that Gnosticism checks many of the boxes, but it occurs too late in history and does not include everything that Paul described in his Colossian letter.

After reviewing about 200 years worth of biblical scholarship, one theologian reported almost four dozen different opinions for the identity of the so-called "Colossian Heresy." He also concluded that the biblical writers were not fighting a known foe called Gnosticism. [House] As we look at the various symptoms which Paul described in his letter, it is almost impossible for such diverse elements to hold together in a single system of worldly philosophy or religious heresy.

Another Bible scholar provided a cogent warning to pastors and teachers who seek to share a valid interpretation of Colossians. This scholar expressed it in these words:

> In attempting to reconstruct the situation behind Paul's writings, the danger of circularity is inevitable. It is all too easy to use what hints there are in a letter to build a false picture of events, and then to read that picture back into the text. ... One must be cautious about constructing too much on the basis of Paul's warnings in chapter 2. ... Exhortation to avoid a certain course of action does not necessarily indicate that those addressed have already fallen prey to the temptation. ... It seems more likely that Paul is issuing a warning than an accusation. ... His language does not suggest that he regards them as in danger of apostasy. [Hooker, 317-319]

I have personally struggled with some of these challenges, and I certainly don't feel like I'm qualified to be dogmatic about this issue. I've decided to stick to the text of the Bible and to say what the text says about the situation in Colossae. I clearly understand that Paul sees a set of potential pitfalls which could derail the faith of this young church. The dangers are real and the Holy Spirit led Paul to warn the Colossians (and us) against turning away from the truths of God's Word.

One alternative we have as we attempt to put together all of the pieces of this puzzle is that the puzzle pieces may not be from a single picture. It could be that there were several trends in the culture of that day which Paul was led to warn believers about. It's possible that their attackers were coming at them from several directions, so they needed to be aware of potential dangers from several sources.

Regardless of whether there was a single "Colossian Heresy," the truths Paul has shared so far – as well as the important things he will share in the upcoming sections – should keep us focused on carefully studying the words of the biblical text using the traditional grammatical-historical method of interpretation to draw out accurate meanings and applications from the book of Colossians. There is plenty of important truth there already, without adding speculations which may not be accurate.

As we end this chapter, let's look for ways to apply these truths. Are there activities in our spiritual life or our church life which we participate in because we think those things are required to maintain our relationship with Christ? These may involve matters of food or drink, special days or rituals, harsh treatment of the body, fear of demonic spirits, or other traditions of men. If you have put your faith and trust in Christ alone for your eternal destiny, then there is nothing that can separate you from Him. God cannot love you any more than He already does right now. Don't allow yourself to be in bondage to man-made rituals which hinder rather than help your connection to Christ.

On the other side of the coin, are you standing in judgment over other believers because they are observing or failing to observe certain things that you think are important? Are your expectations really that important? Are they essential things or are they non-essentials of the faith? Let's exercise more grace as we deal with each other in the family of God.

Right Ways to Master the Flesh: Part One

(Colossians 3:1-10)

In the last chapter we saw how the apostle Paul described the wrong ways to gain mastery over our sin nature. It is important to know about the things the world recommends for mastering our flesh, whether through legalism or mysticism or asceticism. If we're aware of those worldly methods it will help us to avoid them. In today's passage Paul will begin to explain the right ways to gain mastery over our sin nature.

Before we begin, we should ask why it's necessary for a believer in Christ to deal with the sin nature at all. When we put our faith in Christ and received His salvation, didn't that give us a new nature? The answer is yes, believers do have a new spiritual nature that's capable of pleasing God. But we do not yet have our glorified bodies, so we still have the old fleshly nature which coexists with our new spiritual nature. In his earlier letter to the church in Rome, Paul described his own personal struggle with his old nature.

> For I know that nothing good dwells in me, that is, in my flesh; for the willing is present in me, but the doing of the good is not. For the good that I want, I do not do, but I practice the very evil that I do not want. ... I find then the principle that evil is present in me, the one who wants to do good. ... but I see a different law in the members of my body, waging war against the law of my mind and making me a prisoner of the law of sin which is in my members. (Romans 7:18-23)

Putting our trust in Christ for salvation does not neutralize or eradicate the old fleshly nature. Our old nature still exerts a powerful pull toward the old habit patterns that we've developed through years of living apart from God. Those old habits and behavior patterns can only be overruled through the work of the new nature as it submits to the Holy Spirit and obeys the Word of God. One Bible commentator expressed it this way:

> Don't be deceived into thinking that your old mind has been changed because you have been born into the family of God. The mind we have read about in Scripture is the mind we receive by physical birth. We possess within ourselves the same capacity for carnality, vanity, fleshly defilement, corruption, enmity, and attention to earthly, material things that characterized us before we were born into God's family. And if that old mind is allowed to exercise itself, that mind will produce words and actions that are in keeping with the corruption, defilement, blindness, and deadness God says characterizes the mind of the unsaved. However, it is biblical to understand that in the area of mind, the Christian has two capacities—the capacity for divine things through the new mind, and the capacity for carnal, fleshly, sinful, dead things through the old mind. And there is a constant, ceaseless, incessant, unrelenting opposition from the old mind to the new mind as it seeks to glorify God. [Pentecost]

So, this tendency or pull of the fleshly nature in the believer is what the apostle Paul will deal with in today's passage. The chapter and verse divisions in the Bible are not part of the inspired text, and this is one example where the chapter division might imply that an entirely new subject is being introduced. In fact, however, we see from the very first word that what Paul will discuss in this chapter is directly connected to what he has said before.

Col 3:1 - Therefore if you have been raised up with Christ, keep seeking the things above, where Christ is, seated at the right hand of God.

Paul begins this section with the word **therefore** which indicates that what he is about to say is linked to what he already said in the previous verses. We could phrase it, "Therefore, since none of those worldly methods in chapter 2 have any value for mastering the flesh, you must seek help from a different direction."

We saw in Col 1:22 that Christ "reconciled you in His fleshly body through death." Jesus physically died and then was raised from the dead on the third day. But in Col 2:13 Paul made it clear that we were dead, too. He said, "You were dead in your transgressions and the uncircumcision of your flesh." As one commentator expressed it:

> Whereas the Saviour was actually dead and then raised to life, sinners are dead by reason of their sins, unable to please God by responding to His will and not caring to respond. ... The same power which wrought in Christ to raise Him from the dead has brought life out of death to these believers. They have been raised together with Christ. [Harrison, 61]

In Col 2:11-13 Paul introduced the pictures of circumcision and baptism which, as we discussed previously, involves a believer's public identification with the death, burial, and resurrection of Christ. Paul had said that believers were "buried with Him in baptism, in which you were also raised up with Him through faith in the working of God."

Having introduced the image of baptism, Paul applied that picture to the practical issue of how believers are to respond to worldly ways for attempting to control the indulgences of the flesh. In Col 2:20-21 he said, "If you have died with Christ to the elementary principles of the world, why, as if you were living in the world, do you submit yourself to its decrees?" In that passage Paul pictured our death with Christ to show that we are no longer obligated to respond to fleshly desires as we did before. Now we have a choice. We can consider ourselves dead to those desires. This was something which we were not able to do before our salvation.

It is because of our death with Christ, as well as the power of God which raised us to new life, that we now have the ability to overrule or countermand our fleshly desires. Col 2:20 contained the first part of the sequence when it stated: "If you have died with Christ," and now here in Col 3:1 we see the corresponding resurrection which completes the sequence. One Bible commentator has said, "The argument is, that there was such a union between Christ and his people, that by virtue of his death they become dead to sin; that by virtue of his resurrection they rise to spiritual life, and that, therefore, as Christ now lives in heaven, they should live for heaven, and fix their affections there." [Barnes]

Once again, as in Col 2:20, Paul used a Greek first class conditional clause here when he said, "if you have been raised up with Christ." Because we know that our resurrection to new life in Christ is an accomplished fact (Col 2:12-13), we could legitimately translate this, "**Since** you have been raised up with Christ." The last part of this verse is possible only because this condition is in fact true.

So Paul is saying, "Since you have been raised up with Christ, keep seeking the things above." The verb is a present active imperative in the second person plural, so Paul is issuing a command for all of his readers (including us) to be continually or habitually **seeking the things above**. The Greek word *zēteō* means "to diligently pursue something in order to obtain it." This verse commands us to do this. Believers have the help of the indwelling Holy Spirit, of course, but we are to take this action. The Holy Spirit enables, but we must cooperate by doing what is commanded.

What are these things above? How high do our thoughts need to reach? Paul is asking us to stretch ourselves to the limit by seeking the highest heights. We are to seek the place where Christ is. And Paul does not leave us in doubt about where Christ is right now. He reminds us that Christ is seated at the right hand of God in heaven. Upon His ascension

Christ sat down at the right hand of God, as it says in Mark 16:19 – "So then, when the Lord Jesus had spoken to them, He was received up into heaven and sat down at the right hand of God."

The writer of the book of Hebrews echoes what Paul says here. Heb 12:2 tells us to "fix our eyes on Jesus, the author and perfecter of faith, who for the joy set before Him endured the cross, despising the shame, and has sat down at the right hand of the throne of God." One of the things that Jesus is doing for us right now is explained in Rom 8:34 – "Christ Jesus is He who died, yes, rather who was raised, who is at the right hand of God, who also intercedes for us." Jesus is actively at work on our behalf, even from His place in heaven.

How are we to keep seeking the things above? What is the best way to do this? The Greek word **seeking** (*zēteō*) can also mean "to seek in order to find out by thinking." So in the next verse Paul tells us that this process involves the best use of our mind for controlling our thought life.

Col 3:2 - Set your mind on the things above, not on the things that are on earth.

When Paul says **set your mind** it is a translation of the single Greek verb *phroneō* which has the basic meaning: "to think." This verb is also a present active imperative in the second person plural. Paul is telling the Colossians (and all of) us to continually keep on controlling our thoughts. One commentator has said, "You must not only seek heaven, you must think heaven" [Vincent]. As in the previous verse, we are to take this action. The Holy Spirit enables, but we are responsible to do what is commanded.

Sometimes it may seem as if our thoughts have a mind of their own, or that thoughts arise over which we have no control. But that is not true – thoughts do not have a life of their own. Paul is telling us that our thoughts are not independent and uncontrollable.

When fleshly thoughts rise to the surface, as they naturally will even for a believer, the first step is to recognize them. Once we become aware of them, we can evaluate them. If they are fleshly or unworthy thoughts, we need to resist them and replace them by refocusing our attention on things above. One commentator has expressed it this way:

> From now on the Christian will see everything in the light and against the background of eternity. He will no longer live as if this world was all that mattered; he will see this world against the background of the larger world of eternity. ... He will, for instance, put giving above getting, serving above ruling, forgiving above avenging. The Christian will see things, not as they appear to the world, but as they appear to God. [Constable]

Before a person's salvation in Christ, not much thought was given to eternity or the things of God, and there was no enabling power to resist fleshly or worldly ideas. But now a believer is able to focus on things above rather than solely on earthly things. We can bring the priorities of heaven to our earthly lives, centering our focus on things that will matter for eternity.

Since Christ is seated at the right hand of God, He certainly has the power and authority to help us with anything we encounter in our daily lives. Jesus is seated there because He defeated the forces of evil that would try to influence us to indulge our fleshly passions (Col 2:15). As one commentator expressed it, Paul was saying that "life in this world will be better if it is lived by a power beyond this world, the power of the resurrected, ascended, glorified Christ." [BKC]

Paul gives the command to "set your mind on the things above, not on the things that are on earth" and this assumes that it must be possible for a believer to do this. He would not command something that's not possible. This does not mean that it will be easy to do this. There may be times of struggle and failure, but there is forgiveness and restoration for the believer. The truth Paul presents here is that believers are responsible for managing their thought life. We must decide to do this, and this may involve overruling fleshly desires that are loudly clamoring for attention and which we have been in the habit of giving in to for years and years.

Col 3:3 - For you have died and your life is hidden with Christ in God.

The word **for** means that Paul is giving an explanation for what he just commanded. The reason for refusing to respond to fleshly desires is that we are dead, and a dead person is no longer able to give in to sin. Here in this verse Paul tells believers that they are dead ... but alive. This may seem confusing and contradictory until we understand the specific sphere for both our death and our life. As one commentator put it: "The contrast is between the believers' former state, in which they were alive to the world but dead to God, and their present state, in which they are dead to the world but alive to God." [JFB] Before His betrayal and crucifixion Jesus prayed to the Father for His disciples. He said, "I do not ask You to take them out of the world, but to keep them from the evil one" (John 17:15). Believers are to be "in the world" but no longer ruled by worldly passions.

We need to set our minds on things above where our life is hidden with Christ, rather than allowing earthly, fleshly thoughts to dominate our minds and drag us down. As believers we have the option of considering ourselves to be dead to worldly things. We are no longer obligated to obey or be ruled by worldly thoughts and passions. Our position is in Christ, who is our source of true life. Since we have not yet been completely removed from the world, we must live here in these fleshly bodies for a little while longer. But what really matters to us is hidden with Christ as He sits at God's right hand.

The word **hidden** is the Greek word *kruptō* which sounds a lot like the modern English term "crypto." It means "to be kept securely out of sight." First of all, our true life is kept secure in Christ. As one commentator said,

> Your life is with the Redeemer, and he is in the presence of God; and thus nothing can reach it or take it away. It is not left with us, or intrusted to our keeping - for then it might be lost as we might lose a valuable jewel; or it might be taken from us; or we might be defrauded of it; but it is now laid up far out of our sight, and far from the reach of all our enemies. Our eternal life, therefore, is as secure as it could possibly be. The true condition of the Christian is that he is "dead" to this world, but that he has immortal life in view, and that is secure, being in the holy keeping of his Redeemer, now in the presence of God. From this it follows that he should regard himself as living for heaven. [Barnes]

The other aspect of being hidden is that those around us in the world cannot see our new source of life. It is invisible to them, and they can't see any reason why we behave the way we do. As believers, most of the things that attract us and delight us belong to heaven rather than to earth. Our choices and values and motives now come from a heavenly perspective rather than an earthly one. This may not make any sense to the watching world.

Col 3:4 - When Christ, who is our life, is revealed, then you also will be revealed with Him in glory.

The important point which Paul reminds us of here is that Christ is our life. As he said before, we are dead ... but alive, and Christ is our life. He is our Creator, our Redeemer, our Advocate, and the One who holds us together so that we don't fly apart in a puff of smoke. He is the source of our new life, which gives us the desire and power to say "No" to fleshly indulgence and to follow His example in living a life that is pleasing to God. We need this reminder on a moment by moment basis.

This verse also presents a contrast to the previous verse. In verse 3 Paul described our present situation, where the source of our spiritual life is hidden from those in the world. Here verse 4 looks forward to that future time when Jesus comes for us and reveals believers in our glorified state. This brings up a question: When are believers glorified? I'd like to take a short detour here to talk about this issue.

When are believers glorified? In one sense believers are already glorified. In His high-priestly prayer for His disciples before His crucifixion, Jesus said, "The glory which You have given Me I have given to them" (John 17:22). The apostle Paul affirmed this when he wrote to the church in Rome that believers are already glorified (Rom 8:30). Our glorification is an accomplished fact from God's perspective, but we are waiting for its manifestation on that day when Jesus appears and will bring us with Him to the Father's house where He has been preparing a place for us (John 14:3).

The reason we must receive our glorified bodies on that day is because, as Paul told the Corinthian church, "flesh and blood cannot inherit the kingdom of God; nor does the perishable inherit the imperishable" (1 Cor 15:50). If we are to accompany Jesus to His Father's house, then we cannot do it without our glorified bodies. Paul added this explanation in writing to the Corinthians: "It is sown a perishable body, it is raised an imperishable body; it is sown in dishonor, it is raised in glory; it is sown in weakness, it is raised in power; it is sown a natural body, it is raised a spiritual body." (1 Cor 15:42-44) Having a glorified body is a necessity for accompanying Christ to the place He has prepared for us in the presence of the Father.

But when will this happen? Again, in his letter to the Corinthians Paul revealed a mystery that had not been previously recorded in the Old Testament. Paul provided new information about the resurrection of Church-age believers. At the moment when Jesus returns for His own there will be living believers who will be resurrected along with those Church-age saints who have already died. Paul says, "Behold, I tell you a mystery; we will not all sleep, but we will all be changed, in a moment, in the twinkling of an eye, at the last trumpet; for the trumpet will sound, and the dead will be raised imperishable, and we will be changed. For this perishable must put on the imperishable, and this mortal must put on immortality." (1 Cor 15:51-53)

What Paul said in 1 Cor 15 sounds very much like another passage in his first letter to the church at Thessalonica. There he said, "For the Lord Himself will descend from heaven with a shout, with the voice of the archangel and with the trumpet of God, and the dead in Christ will rise first. Then we who are alive and remain will be caught up together with them in the clouds to meet the Lord in the air, and so we shall always be with the Lord." (1 Thess 4:16-17) These passages are referring to what is called the Rapture of the Church. This is the moment when Jesus will appear above the earth to gather the members of His body, the Church, and to remove them from the earth. The Church will depart with Christ to be with Him in the Father's house. That is the moment in time when Church-age believers will receive their glorified bodies.

This is what Paul refers to in several places in Colossians chapter 1. Verse 5 calls this "the hope laid up for you in heaven." He also mentioned it in verse 22 as the time when Jesus will "present you before Him holy and blameless and beyond reproach." And according to the mystery that Paul shared in verse 27, believers have this hope of glory. The time when believers will receive their glorified body is a wonderful truth, but we shouldn't lose sight of Paul's main point in Col 3:4, which is that Christ is our life now. It is only by living by the values and priorities of Christ in the power of the indwelling Holy Spirit that we have any hope of mastering the flesh.

Col 3:5 - Therefore consider the members of your earthly body as dead to immorality, impurity, passion, evil desire, and greed, which amounts to idolatry.

A more literal translation would be, "Kill therefore your earthly members." Many English translations follow this literal wording. Most use the phrase "put to death" (ASV, CSB, ESV, NET, NIV, NKJV, NLT, RSV) while the KJV says "mortify your earthly members." The single Greek verb *nekroō* is translated "**put to death**" and it can also mean "to deprive something of its power." The verb form is an aorist active imperative, which is often used to express the urgent need to take immediate action. As in the previous verses, we are to take this action. The Holy Spirit enables us, but we are responsible to do what is commanded. What does it mean to "put to death?" One theologian expressed it this way:

> Death always means separation, never extinction, so putting to death the deeds of the body cannot mean eradicating them. That doesn't happen in this life. But it does mean separating myself from these things. ... Death to self is not extinction of the self-life, but separation from its power. So putting to death the deeds of the body does not mean that those deeds will no longer be a part of our existence, but it can mean that they no longer need to be part of our experience. [Ryrie-B, 197]

The New American Standard Bible (NAS95) translated this verse to include the involvement of our minds as part of the process, similar to verse 2 which says, "set your mind on the things above, not on the things that are on earth." So it says we are to consider our fleshly passions to be dead. If indeed we died, then we must treat the members of our body as dead and unable to respond.

One pastor shared a story about two sisters who were in the habit of attending wild parties where they would engage in all kinds of worldly activities. But these sisters became Christians and found new life in Christ. Some time later they received an invitation to another of those raucous parties, and they sent their RSVP in these words: "We regret that we cannot attend because we recently died." [Wiersbe, 133]

Here in verse 5 Paul begins with the word **therefore**, so we could say, "Because we have died and our life is hidden with Christ in God," we are to consider the members of our earthly bodies to be dead to the sins of the flesh. This is similar to the way Paul expressed the same idea in his earlier letter to the church in Rome. Paul's earlier teaching would have been circulated among the churches, so it's quite possible that Paul would have expected the Colossians to be familiar with this important truth. Similar to the wording we see in Colossians, Rom 6:11-13 says, "consider yourselves to be dead to sin, but alive to God in Christ Jesus. Therefore do not let sin reign in your mortal body so that you obey its lusts, and do not go on presenting the members of your body to sin as instruments of unrighteousness; but present yourselves to God as those alive from the dead, and your members as instruments of righteousness to God." One commentator expressed it this way:

> In an earlier letter the apostle indicated a secret which greatly aids in reaching this objective, namely, to reckon oneself to be dead to sin (Rom 6:11). Sin is illogical, irrational, inconceivable for a dead man. ... In principle the sinful nature has been crucified with the Lord, but there remains the necessity of acting on that fact by refusing to give sin any right to continue its mastery over the life that Christ has purchased by His precious blood. ... To bear this in mind when sin (which is far from dead to us) seeks to allure us is a big help toward achieving deliverance from its power. [Harrison, 78]

When Paul says "consider the members of your earthly body as dead," we understand that the members of the body themselves are merely instruments that are used to engage in fleshly activities. Our body parts can be used for evil purposes or to accomplish good things. As Paul said initially, it is our mindset which controls how our body parts will be used.

Now that Paul has explained how believers are to deal with our fleshly passions, he goes on to mention several examples of the most common and devastating things which believers are exposed to in the world. He lists immorality, impurity, passion, evil desire, and greed, which amounts to idolatry. These are sensual sins. Let's look at them one by one.

Immorality (*porneia*, from which we get the English word pornography) is a general or broad term that refers to any type of sexual activity outside of the marriage relationship. Different aspects of sexual activity were often included in the worship of pagan deities during their temple rituals, so *porneia* was very common in the culture of Paul's day. And as we look at our society today, we would have to conclude that *porneia* is just as common in our culture as it was in Paul's time.

Impurity (*akatharsia*) literally means the opposite of clean, either in a physical or moral sense. It can refer to any unnatural, filthy, or unapproved sensual action, whether done by oneself or with others, and it includes the idea of perversion. Synonyms include defilement, foulness, and wantonness.

Passion (*pathos*) is a general term that literally means "a feeling which the mind suffers." It can have both good and bad connotations, and in the New Testament it is used three times, all with a negative connotation. Here in Colossians it means "lustful desire that does not rest until it is satisfied." 1 Thess 4:5 calls it "lustful passion," and Rom 1:26 translates it "degrading or dishonorable passion." As one scholar said, "Pathos is the soul's diseased condition out of which the various lusts spring. These are lusts that dishonor those who indulge in them." [Zodhiates]

Evil desire (*epithumia*) is an insatiable longing for what is forbidden. It is a lust to satisfy fleshly appetites and carnal desires. The list that Paul gives here seems to be moving from the most specific sensual actions to the more general sensual attitudes. "Evil desire" goes beyond actions to include the evil thoughts or intentions of the mind.

Greed (*pleonexia*) is a compound word from *pleiōn* ("more or greater") and *echō* ("to have"). So it literally means "to have more" of anything, in either a good or bad sense. It has a wider and more intense meaning than the English word greed. It denotes a radical disposition to have more, a "grasping selfishness that has grown into a passion." In the context here it seems to carry the thought of never having enough sensual indulgence. The sensual desires of the flesh are insatiable, and Paul goes even further by saying that they amount to idolatry. They can be worshiped and served in the place which God should hold in our lives. One commentator expressed it this way:

> It is hard to resist the suggestion that covetousness is linked here with sexual immorality, and so speaks of the greed which seeks its satisfaction in what is not lawful. ... This sin is idolatrous, for it concentrates the whole being upon something other than God. It is characteristic of sexual indulgence that it leads to an unhealthy, and ultimately perverted, obsession. This can be seen not only on an individual level, but also in a community. When godliness is rejected and the lust of the flesh encouraged, it is not long before sex is worshiped instead of God. [Carson, 82]

As we come to the end of this list of sensual sins, we need to remember what Paul said we are to do with them. He told us that we must "consider the members of your earthly body" to be dead to all of these fleshly sins and sensual attitudes. We are to fully separate from them, through a radical shift in our mental focus and our behavior.

In the next two verses Paul will give a powerful reason for what he has just said.

Col 3:6-7 - For it is because of these things that the wrath of God will come upon the sons of disobedience, 7 and in them you also once walked, when you were living in them.

Here Paul provides an important motivation for mastering our fleshly nature. He says that the sensual sins listed in the last verse (and others like them) are bringing the wrath of God upon those who engage in them. **Wrath** (*orgē*) is the righteous indignation or anger of God which manifests itself in punishment for sin. To participate in these sins invites the wrath of God. Because the world ignores God and loves this kind of sensual lifestyle, people who continue in these sins are simply compounding their condemnation.

One way in which the wrath of God can be evident in this life is that God may simply allow people to continue living in their sinful lifestyle. As it says in Rom 1:24-32, He "gives them over" to their self-destructive ways and sadly allows them to destroy themselves. Ultimately, however, God's wrath and judgment will fall on all the sons of disobedience. A quick survey shows that God's wrath is predicted almost a dozen times in the Gospels, over twenty times in the New Testament epistles, and throughout the book of Revelation. There will be no escape for unbelievers from God's ultimate wrath to come.

Paul wrote to the Thessalonian church that God rescues believers from the wrath to come (1 Thess 1:10). And as Paul said in Col 1:10, believers are meant to "walk in a manner worthy of the Lord, to please Him in all respects." But participating in the sensual sins that Paul listed will have exactly the opposite effect. God hates these sins and He is compelled to judge, condemn, and punish people for them, even if they are believers. So even though a believer will ultimately be rescued from the wrath to come, sin always has consequences. The last verse of this chapter contains a clear warning which we will discuss in context when we get to it, but that warning is a general principle which applies here to believers who participate in the sensual sins. In Col 3:25 Paul writes, "For he who does wrong will receive the consequences of the wrong which he has done, and that without partiality." This goes for believers as well as for unbelievers. Sinful attitudes and behaviors will incur a judgment from God, and He shows no partiality. This is a powerful motivation for believers to reject and avoid the sensual sins and the pull of our old nature toward fleshly indulgence in any area of life.

In verse 7 Paul gives a second reason for the Colossian believers (and us) to avoid the sins of the flesh. He reminds them that they themselves were once enslaved to those sins in their life before salvation. As Paul had said in Col 1:21, "You were formerly alienated and hostile in mind, engaged in evil deeds." Since God rescued them out of that pitiful condition, it would make no sense to return to that empty and destructive way of life. They left that kind of life behind and should be determined never to revisit it. One commentator explained it like this:

> Do believers in local churches commit such sins? Unfortunately, they sometimes do. Each of the New Testament epistles sent to local churches makes mention of these sins and warns against them. I am reminded of a pastor who preached a series of sermons against the sins of the saints. A member of his congregation challenged him one day, saying that it would be better if the pastor preached those messages to the lost. The church member said, "Sin in the life of a Christian is different from sin in the lives of other people." The pastor replied, "Yes ... it's worse!" [Wiersbe, 135]

So, after warning believers about sensual sins in verses 5-7, Paul will now list examples of what we might call relational sins.

Col 3:8 - But now you also, put them all aside: anger, wrath, malice, slander, and abusive speech from your mouth.

Paul begins this verse with an emphatic contrast – **But now**. He is saying, "Yes, you once lived in those sins, but now 'you have died and your life is hidden with Christ in God,' (Col 3:3) so you now have the ability to put aside all of these things." The Greek verb translated **put them aside** is *apotithēmi* which means "to put off and lay aside, as when removing soiled clothing." Once again, we are to take this action. The Holy Spirit enables, but we are responsible to do what is commanded. This picture of changing one's clothing may imply that it would be an easy task to put all of these things aside, but that is not the case. All of these things are deeply ingrained in our fleshly nature, so it may require deliberate and sometimes painful decisions on our part through the power of the indwelling Holy Spirit to keep these things from rearing their ugly heads. These so-called relational sins involve both our attitudes and our actions.

Anger (*orgē*). We saw this word in verse 6 where it was used for the righteous indignation or anger of God toward sin. Here in the present context, however, it is not being applied to a righteous God but to flawed human beings. Here it indicates a fleshly attitude of indignation which has a hint of entitlement and bitterness over unmet self-centered expectations.

Wrath (*thumos*) is a sudden and passionate outburst of anger or irritation. One language expert said, "It refers to a burning anger which flares up and burns with the intensity of a fire." Believers are called to exercise self-control, and not allow themselves to give vent to angry impulses when they rise to the surface (James 1:9).

Malice (*kakia*) is an evil habit of mind or an attitude of ill will that is determined to do harm to others. If we have malice toward someone, we will be sad when he is successful, and we will rejoice when he has trouble. [Wiersbe]

Slander (*blasphēmia*) expresses itself in a habit of verbal abuse against someone, which is intended to damage someone's reputation by spreading evil reports. Synonyms include backbiting, reviling, defaming, insulting others, or gossiping about others.

Abusive speech (*aischrologia*) literally means to "say filthy things." It is used in this verse to mean that people who have been redeemed by Christ should never allow shameful or filthy words to come out of their mouth. A Christian ought to use a different vocabulary than he used in his life before salvation. We must think before we speak (Eph 5:4) and bridle the tongue (James 1:26). Paul adds one more sin to the list, and that is lying.

Col 3:9 - Do not lie to one another, since you laid aside the old self with its evil practices,

Do not **lie** (*pseudomai*) is a command in the present tense, which could be translated, "stop being in the habit of lying to one another." It means "to speak falsely or deceitfully." Here Paul includes any misrepresentation of the truth that is intended to deceive someone in order to gain something for ourselves or to make ourselves look better than we are. Unfortunately this is one of the easiest indulgences of the flesh for a believer to fall into. It is so ingrained in our nature, and we have practiced it for so long, that it has become a habitual way of speaking to others.

If we add lying to the list, then there are six examples of the relational sins which Paul tells us to lay aside. In verse 8 Paul used the verb *apotithēmi* which means "to put off and lay aside." But here in verse 9 the same phrase **"laid aside"** is the way the creators of the NASB chose to render an even more powerful word. This is actually the same word Paul had used in Col 2:15 when he said that God "disarmed the rulers and authorities, making a public display of them." The Greek word *apekduomai* is a double compound word, created by combining the words *apoduō* and *ekduō*. Paul used this term to express how completely the rulers and authorities had been stripped of their power, so here he uses the same word to express how completely believers should strip their old nature of its power over them.

"The old self with its evil practices" is Paul's way of referring to the fleshly, sinful nature that he has been talking about throughout this entire section. This is a powerful image of the believer conquering or mastering the habits and passions of the old self. For the word "old" he used the Greek term *palaios* which means "ancient, worn by use and the worse for wear."

The fact is, though, that "laying aside the old self" is only half of the picture. The other part of the process is described in the next verse.

Col 3:10 - and have put on the new self who is being renewed to a true knowledge according to the image of the One who created him--

Not only are we to put off the old self, here Paul says we also need to put on the new self. This is the principle of replacement. To **put on** is the Greek word *enduō* which literally means "to go under, be plunged into, or to sink into" something. It was commonly used for the act of putting on clothing, but the word itself hints at something similar to what happens during believers' baptism.

There are two different Greek words for "**new**." One is *kainos* which means "new in kind or character." The other word is *neos* which means "new in time; fresh or young." Here Paul used the word *neos* which he places in direct contrast to the old, ancient, well-worn self. The new self is the one that was recently received at the moment of salvation. It is a believer's fresh new life that is "hidden with Christ in God" (Col 3:3).

Paul says here that this new life is itself in the process of being continually refreshed. The phrase "**being renewed**" is the Greek word *anakainoō* which has the second Greek word for "new" as its root. So Paul is using both Greek words for "new" to show that our new life is both new in time, fresh, and unspoiled but also new in quality or character. As one language expert said, "Paul adds the meaning of kainos to that of neos. It is a continual refreshment (*kainos*) of the new man (*neos*)." [RWP]

As we have seen previously in Col 1:9-10 and Col 2:2, this process of continuous renewal and spiritual growth involves increasing in true knowledge. The single Greek word translated here as "**true knowledge**" (*epignosis*) is the same word used in those earlier verses, and we recall that it means much more than simply knowing something. It carries the idea of thoroughly understanding, of recognizing the importance, of accepting and applying something personally in our lives. Believers grow in knowledge through the ministry of the Word of God. As we read the Bible and hear sound biblical teaching, the indwelling Holy Spirit applies that knowledge to our lives. As one commentator said, "The Word of God is the food that fuels the growth of the new self. How believers grow depends on how much knowledge they put into practice in their lives." [MacArthur, 150]

Now, Paul adds that as we grow spiritually we also become more like our Creator. As he says here, the believer is gradually conformed to the image of the One who created him. This is similar to what Paul had written earlier to the church in Rome, "Those whom He foreknew, He also predestined to become conformed to the image of His Son" (Rom 8:29). Our spiritual growth leads to increasing Christ-likeness. One commentator expressed it this way:

> The image of God which the new man bears from the beginning in a rudimentary form, and which is continually imprinting itself more deeply upon him, has for its principal feature holiness. ... This is the goal of all our putting off the old and putting on the new. This is the ultimate purpose of God, in all His self-revelation. For this purpose Christ has come and died and lives. For this purpose the Spirit of God dwells in us. This is the immortal hope with which we may encourage our souls in our often weary struggles, that our poor sinful natures may be transformed into that wondrous likeness. [Expositors]

By way of summary, in this chapter we've seen why it's necessary for a believer in Christ to deal with his sin nature. Putting our trust in Christ for salvation did not neutralize or eradicate our old fleshly nature. That old nature still exerts a powerful pull toward sinful habit patterns. But since we have been raised up with Christ, we now have the ability to say "No" to the old attitudes and behaviors, and we can seek to use the things above as our new pattern for living.

God commands us to set our minds on the things above, not on earthly things, so believers are responsible before God for managing their thought life. By considering ourselves to be dead to the sins of the flesh, we separate ourselves from them and are no longer obligated to give in to them. Paul listed several examples of sensual sins, which bring the wrath of God on those who participate in them. And he also listed examples of relational sins that result from fleshly attitudes and ways of speaking to others.

Even though it may be painful and difficult at times, we now have the power through the indwelling Holy Spirit to separate from the sins which are so deeply ingrained in our fleshly nature. Using the principle of replacement, we can put off the old ways and put on the new ways which please God. This process of continuous renewal and spiritual growth involves increasing our knowledge of who God is and how we can be conformed to His image by living according to the principles of His Word.

Right Ways to Master the Flesh: Part Two

(Colossians 3:11-17)

In this section we will see how Paul concludes his message about the believer's task of mastering the old fleshly nature. In the previous sections he wrote about several wrong ways to master the flesh, and he also focused on the fleshly attitudes and behaviors that believers are to "put off" or "put away" from themselves. There were both sensual sins and relational sins that we are to consider ourselves as "dead" to. Since believers have been raised up with Christ, we now have the ability to say "No" to old attitudes and behaviors, and we can seek to use the things above as our new pattern for living. Growing in Christ-likeness is possible now because we are in Christ and have the indwelling Holy Spirit who gives us the desire and power to please Him.

The principle of replacement means that when we put off the old ways we must then put on the new ways which please God. In the last section we saw many examples of things that a believer must put off, so to complete the replacement, in this section Paul will explain what a believer must put on. On the heels of Paul's list of relational sins, today's passage mentions several social, racial, and class distinctions which were an integral part of the society of Paul's day.

Col 3:11 - a renewal in which there is no distinction between Greek and Jew, circumcised and uncircumcised, barbarian, Scythian, slave and freeman, but Christ is all, and in all.

Social norms required people to behave differently toward others based on the kinds of distinctions mentioned in this verse. But here Paul tells us that these distinctions should not exist in the body of Christ. We can consider these distinctions and prejudices to be part of the social sins that Paul had just condemned.

The first part of this verse can be translated literally as, "Where not exists Greek and Jew." Obviously that sounds pretty rough in English, but several Bible versions follow this closely. Some say, "Where there is neither Greek nor Jew" (ASV, KJV, NKJV) while others say, "Here there is no Greek or Jew" (ESV, NET, NIV, RSV). Any word-for-word translation of the Bible will probably use one of these renderings, because to say more than that would be to go beyond translation into the area of interpretation. The question is, when Paul says "Where there is neither Greek nor Jew," where is "where?" – what is the area or sphere being referred to?

The Christian Standard Bible (CSB) says, "In Christ there is not Greek and Jew." That version has chosen to identify Christ as the sphere in which there is no distinction between Greek and Jew. This makes sense because throughout this letter believers are said to be "in Christ" (Col 1:2, 28; 2:6-7, 10-11; 3:3), and the end of this verse states that "Christ is all, and in all."

The New American Standard Bible (NAS95) and the Legacy Standard Bible (LSB) both translate the verse by connecting it to the idea of renewal in the previous verse. Col 3:9-10 say, "you laid aside the old self with its evil practices, and have put on the new self who is being renewed." So we might paraphrase this by saying, "As believers are being renewed and continue to grow in spiritual maturity, they understand that these social, racial, and class distinctions are meaningless within the body of Christ, the Church." This way of understanding the verse also makes sense. But it seems important to point out that these Bible versions have gone beyond a strict word-for-word translation and have ventured into the realm of interpretation.

Throughout the ages various people groups have formed their identities around their commonalities. This has led to an "us versus them" mentality in different parts of societies across the globe and throughout history. The interesting thing that began to happen in Paul's day, though, was that the Church cut across all of these distinctions. People from radically different groups began to be included in the body of Christ. The Church started to erase all of the tenaciously held social norms and class distinctions.

Within the Church there were believers who had been rescued out of cultured Greek society, as well as former members of Judaism. A strict Jewish perspective made the distinction between the circumcised and the uncircumcised, or Jews versus Gentiles. The cultured Greeks made the distinction between themselves and the barbarians – those who were not Greek speakers and whose speech sounded like gibberish to them. There were even some believers who were Scythians, and they were considered to be the worst of the barbarians. Of course, many slaves became believers right alongside the free men from their society. So the Church began to break down cultural norms in the area of social and class distinctions.

The important truth which Paul states at the end of this verse is that "Christ is all, and in all." There is an old saying that "the ground is level at the foot of the cross," which means that there are no distinctions between Christians – all believers are sinners saved by grace. As one commentator said:

Christ absorbs in Himself all distinctions, being to all alike, everything that they need for justification, sanctification, and glorification....The unity of the divine life shared in by all believers, counterbalances all differences, even as great as that between the polished Greek and the crude Scythian. Christianity imparts to all the only source of sound social and moral life. [JFB]

We've seen that Paul has shared wonderful truths about the greatness of Christ throughout this letter. He told us that Christ is fully God, that He is our Redeemer, our Creator, and that "in Him all things hold together" (Col 1:17). Paul was given new revelation for the Church Age, which included "Christ in you, the hope of glory" (Col 1:26-27). Because of the indwelling Christ, we partake of His fullness or completeness (Col 2:10). And just a few verses ago Paul shared that "Christ is our life" (Col 3:4). No wonder he declares here that "Christ is all, and in all."

Now, as a result of all we have in Christ, Paul will begin to describe what believers are to "put on" as we seek to be more like Christ.

Col 3:12 - So, as those who have been chosen of God, holy and beloved, put on a heart of compassion, kindness, humility, gentleness and patience;

We know from the last section that Paul listed many negative examples of both sensual and relational sins which believers were to "put aside," as if they are removing dirty clothing. In order to complete the picture, starting here in this verse Paul will begin to explain the positive and valuable things that believers should "put on" – as if they are replacing old dirty clothing with new, fresh garments.

As we look at the first part of this verse, a literal translation would be, "Clothe yourselves, therefore, as chosen ones of God, holy and beloved." The Greek word order has the verb first in this sentence for emphasis. To **put on** is the word *enduō* which literally means "to go under, be plunged into, or to sink into" something. It was commonly used for the act of putting on clothing, and it is the same word that Paul had used in verse 10 where he said, "put on the new self." The verb form is an imperative or command. The Holy Spirit will empower us if we cooperate with Him, but we are responsible to do what is commanded.

Paul begins by saying, "**therefore**," or "in view of what has just been said." So we could paraphrase this as, "Therefore, since Christ is all and in all, believers are to clothe themselves with all of these qualities." It is because of the unity that such diverse believers have in Christ that they are able to behave graciously toward each other. Very different types of people have all been made part of the family of God, and (contrary to what societal norms might dictate) these diverse peoples are to behave toward one another as brothers and sisters in Christ. One commentator expressed it this way:

> Because Christ is all and in all, therefore, clothe yourselves with all brotherly graces, corresponding to the great unity into which all Christians are brought by their common possession of Christ. The whole field of Christian morality is not covered here, but only some examples that concern the social duties which result from that unity. [Expositors]

Now, before Paul launches into a list of positive qualities, he pauses to give three important descriptions of these believers which should motivate them even more toward gracious behavior because of their unity in Christ.

In the phrase "those who have been chosen of God" the word **chosen** is the Greek word *eklektos* which literally means "selected out of." This thought is similar to what Paul said previously in Col 1:13-14 – "He rescued us out of the domain of darkness, and transferred us into the kingdom of His beloved Son, in whom we have redemption, the forgiveness of sins." The word *eklektos* here emphasizes the fact that God purposely selected each of these very diverse individuals to be members of His body, the Church. If God Himself selected each of them, then who are we to question His choice or to treat others disrespectfully based on societal distinctions?

Next Paul says these believers are **holy** which is the Greek word *hagios*. This is the same word which was translated "saints" four times in chapter one (Col 1:2, 4, 12, and 26). As it did there, here it also means "consecrated or set apart for God." If God Himself consecrated these believers for His own purposes, then who are we to find fault with His decision?

Finally Paul says these believers are **beloved** which is the word *agapaō*. This is the same word translated "love" or "beloved" which Paul has been using throughout this letter. As we learned in an earlier chapter, this type of love is unconditional, and it could be described as unmerited, unselfish, and self-sacrificing. It is the highest form of love and is the kind of love which God Himself expresses toward those He has chosen and consecrated. Again, if God Himself has set His love upon these diverse individuals, then who are we to withhold our love from them? Believers have a unity in Christ which should lead the members of His body to follow His example in viewing different believers as God's own chosen, consecrated, and beloved people. One commentator has said,

> It is most significant to note that every one of the graces listed has to do with personal relationships between people. There is no mention of virtues like efficiency or cleverness, not even of diligence or industry – not that these things are unimportant. But the great basic Christian virtues are those which govern human relationships. [Guzik]

So, Paul now begins to list some of the positive attitudes and behaviors that believers must "put on" in their relationships with others. As we look over this list it becomes apparent that these are all qualities which Jesus Himself exemplified during His earthly life. So believers are literally to become more and more Christ-like by following the example of His behavior.

Put on ... a heart of **compassion** (*oiktirmos*). This describes the sympathetic compassion one shows for the sufferings of others. This is sometimes translated "mercies" and is listed in 2 Cor 1:3 as a character trait of God the Father. Just as God's heart is stirred with pity, our hearts should also respond to the suffering of others – especially to fellow members of the body of Christ.

Kindness (*chrēstotēs*) which, as one lexicon says, is "the grace that pervades a person's nature and mellows all that which would be harsh and severe. It was used to describe wine that has mellowed with age." [Zodhiates] This is the same quality that God demonstrates to us according to Eph 2:7, and Paul listed it in Gal 5:22 as part of the fruit of the Spirit which should be evident in the lives of all believers.

Humility (*tapeinophrosynē*) is lowliness of mind and it means "to have an accurate estimate of one's significance." This is the same word that Paul had used in a negative context in Col 2:18 and 23 where he described the "false humility" of those who were advocating visions and the worship of angels. Here in this verse Paul has the positive connotation in view. Genuine humility is a character quality which God values highly, and the epistles of both Paul and Peter list it among the virtues that believers should cultivate (Eph 4:2; Phil 2:3; 1 Peter 5:5).

Gentleness (*prautēs*) is often translated as "meekness" and it carries the idea of "power under God's control." One lexicon said it is "an attitude of spirit which accepts God's dealings with us as good, and does not dispute or resist. It is a condition of mind and heart which demonstrates gentleness, not in weakness but in power, which is a balance born of strength of character." [Zodhiates] Gentleness is a character quality of Jesus (Matt 11:29), and Paul included this word in Gal 5:23 as part of the fruit of the Spirit which all believers should display.

Patience (*makrothumia*) is a word we have seen before in Col 1:11. It literally means "long tempered" and it can be translated as "longsuffering or forbearance toward people." This word is also included in Gal 5:22 as part of the fruit of the Spirit. Both Paul (1 Tim 1:16) and Peter (2 Peter 3:15) made it clear that this is an important character trait of Jesus Himself which we are to imitate.

Col 3:13 - bearing with one another, and forgiving each other, whoever has a complaint against anyone; just as the Lord forgave you, so also should you.

Bearing with one another (*anechomai*) literally means "to hold oneself up or back" and here in this context it carries the idea of maintaining your own good disposition or behavior in the midst of dealing with something or someone who is difficult. It can be translated "to sustain oneself while having patience with the weaknesses of others." Jesus demonstrated this quality many times. Once when His disciples could not cast out a demon from a child, Jesus said, "You unbelieving and perverse generation, how long shall I be with you and put up with you? Bring your son here" (Luke 9:41). In Eph 4:1-2 Paul implored believers to walk in a manner worthy of their calling, "with all humility and gentleness, with patience, showing tolerance for one another in love." So, depending on the situation, this could mean enduring persecution (1 Cor 4:12), putting up with difficult people, showing tolerance for others, and patiently bearing the weaknesses of others.

When Paul said, **Forgiving each other**, he used the Greek word *charizomai*. This word usually means "giving", especially giving a gift that is unattainable, unrequested, or even undeserved." When it is translated as "forgive" it means that the one to whom a debt is owed "gives" the cancellation of the debt as a gift of grace or unmerited favor. The more common word for forgiving (*aphiēmi*) has the broader meaning of "sending away" but it is not used here. In this verse

Paul seems to be emphasizing the gracious aspect of behavior that believers are to demonstrate toward each other. The goal should be to have a generous and gracious spirit among the believers.

"Whoever has a **complaint** against anyone" uses the Greek word *momphē* which means a fault or something to place blame upon. When fault-finding and accusations are raised between believers, gracious generosity should be the spirit of the response by both parties. In such situations we are to "put off anger, wrath, malice, slander, and abusive speech" and we are to "put on kindness, humility, gentleness, patience, forbearance, and forgiveness." How we respond during conflicts with other believers is a revealing measurement of how well we are putting this section of Colossians into practice in our lives.

At the end of this verse Paul provides a powerful reason why believers are to forgive each other. He says, "just as the Lord forgave you, so also should you." The Lord Jesus Christ graciously canceled your immense debt of sin, so you should follow His example by forgiving the relatively miniscule faults or debts that you feel are owed by a fellow believer. All of these complaints are quite minor in comparison to the life and death matters that you have been forgiven of by Jesus.

This sounds very much like the story Jesus told about the king who was settling accounts with those who owed him money (Matt 18:21-35).

> Then Peter came and said to Him, "Lord, how often shall my brother sin against me and I forgive him? Up to seven times?" Jesus said to him, "I do not say to you, up to seven times, but up to seventy times seven. "For this reason the kingdom of heaven may be compared to a king who wished to settle accounts with his slaves. When he had begun to settle them, one who owed him ten thousand talents was brought to him. [this would be the equivalent of several million dollars today.] But since he did not have the means to repay, his lord commanded him to be sold, along with his wife and children and all that he had, and repay-

ment to be made. So the slave fell to the ground and prostrated himself before him, saying, 'Have patience with me and I will repay you everything.' And the lord of that slave felt compassion and released him and forgave him the debt. But that slave went out and found one of his fellow slaves who owed him a hundred denarii [this about 1/600,000 of what was originally owed]; and he seized him and began to choke him, saying, 'Pay back what you owe.' So his fellow slave fell to the ground and began to plead with him, saying, 'Have patience with me and I will repay you.' But he was unwilling and went and threw him in prison until he should pay back what was owed. So when his fellow slaves saw what had happened, they were deeply grieved and came and reported to their lord all that had happened. Then summoning him, his lord said to him, 'You wicked slave, I forgave you all that debt because you pleaded with me. Should you not also have had mercy on your fellow slave, in the same way that I had mercy on you?' And his lord, moved with anger, handed him over to the torturers until he should repay all that was owed him. My heavenly Father will also do the same to you, if each of you does not forgive his brother from your heart."

So, believers are not to follow the example of the unforgiving servant by quibbling with fellow believers over small matters, because the Lord has canceled their own debt which was so great they could never pay it.

The fact that Paul included toleration and forgiveness in the list of attitudes and behaviors that believers are to "put on" means that there will, at times, be difficulties between believers within the body of Christ. Even though there is a powerful unity in Christ, diversity still exists. There will always be differences between people which will need to be tolerated, and there may be difficulties with others which will need to be forgiven. Believers are all trying to master their old fleshly nature, and some are having more success with that than others. Now Paul adds the grand finale to his list:

Col 3:14 - Beyond all these things put on love, which is the perfect bond of unity.

The word **beyond** translates the Greek preposition *epi* which means "upon or over." So we could view love as the outer garment that believes are to "put on" which encompasses all of the other virtues that we should exemplify. When we think of love as the outer garment we should understand how love functions in believers' relationships. In his earlier letter to the church at Corinth, Paul explained how the absence of this one quality can actually negate all of the others. In 1 Cor 13 Paul said that Christian speech unaccompanied by love becomes nothing more than an irritating noise (v. 1). He said that even if a believer has the gift of prophecy or has all knowledge and all faith, it amounts to nothing without love (v. 2). If a believer gives all his possessions to others, and goes so far as to be martyred for his commitment to Christ, but does not have love, then it is worthless (v. 3). In 1 Cor 13:4-7 Paul showed that love actually does encompass all of the other virtues – it literally binds them all together in perfect unity. One commentator expressed it this way:

> It may be possible for all the dispositions already named to exist in some fashion without love. There might be pity without love. The feeling with which one looks upon some poor outcast, or on some stranger in sorrow, or even on an enemy in misery, may be genuinely compassionate, and yet clearly separate from love. So it is with all the others. There may be kindness without any of the divine emotions, and there may even be forbearance reaching the point of forgiveness, and yet leaving the heart untouched in its deepest recesses. But if these virtues were exercised in the absence of love they would be fragmentary, shallow, and would have no guarantee of effectiveness. Let love come into the heart and knit a man to the poor creature whom he had only pitied before, or to the enemy whom he had at the most been able with an effort to forgive, and it lifts these other emotions into a nobler life. He who pities may not love, but he who loves cannot help but pity, and that pity will flow with a deeper current and be of a purer quality than the shrunken stream which does not rise from that higher source. [Expositors]

This kind of love – God's kind of love – is almost impossible to demonstrate apart from the power of the indwelling Holy Spirit in the life of a believer. We can think of the Holy Spirit as the one who provides the new articles of clothing and then helps us to put on the entire outfit, making sure that it fits perfectly and functions exactly as intended. It is impossible to become more and more Christ-like without the constant help of the Holy Spirit within. One commentator has said,

> The articles of the Christian's attire are enumerated here, and we need to refer to this list often in order to be sure that none of them is missing from our spiritual wardrobe. We must not always focus on the negative of avoiding wrong, because the positive has a clear claim on us; and in each circumstance of trial or temptation we must advance to meet it, clothed in Christ. As the Lord acted, so must we. We must partake of the family likeness. [Meyer]

At the end of this verse Paul said, "love, which is the perfect bond of unity." A literal translation would be "a bond of perfection." **Bond** is the Greek word *sundesmos* which means something which binds or joins things together. In Col 2:19 this same word was translated ligaments in the context of how the body of Christ is held together by the so-called "bands" that join all the parts and keep them all in their right places. So, here in this verse, love functions the same way. Without love, all of the qualities mentioned previously could become "out of joint." This analogy helps us to understand why love is so important for the proper functioning of all these attitudes and behaviors.

The word that is translated **perfect** is the Greek word *teleiotēs* which comes from the word *teleios*. It describes something that has reached its intended goal. It is complete or fully ripened and mature as a unified whole. So, without love, all of the other qualities – as valuable as they are individually – would not be complete. They would not be able to perfectly fulfill their intended goal or purpose. Love is essential to this entire process of growing in Christ-likeness.

This concludes Paul's message about how believers should put off their old fleshly nature while putting on the character of Christ. As one commentator has said,

> So end the frequent references in this letter to putting off the old and putting on the new. The sum of them all is that we must first put on Christ by faith, and then by daily effort clothe our spirits in the graces of character which He gives us, and by which we shall be like Him. [Expositors]

Paul will now go on to add three general instructions which will help believers to live a life that is pleasing to God as they relate to others around them.

Col 3:15 - Let the peace of Christ rule in your hearts, to which indeed you were called in one body; and be thankful.

This sentence begins with the word "and" in the original Greek, so it can be viewed as a follow-up to Paul's command in the last verse. Here he commands them to "let the peace of Christ rule." This kind of **peace** (*eirēnē*) includes the qualities of harmony, tranquility, and calm unity that have their source in Christ. Peace belongs to Christ but believers can partake of His peace just as they can share in all of the other aspects of His fullness (Col 2:10).

Here Paul does not simply say that they are to have this peace. He says they must let peace rule in their lives. **Rule** (*brabeuō*) means "to arbitrate, govern, or control." When you think of something you might select to be in control, do you think of peace? We may have listed forcefulness, or determination, or a commanding presence, or decisiveness, or confidence, but we would probably never have chosen peace to be in charge. But God is telling us that peace is what He wants to rule over our attitudes and behaviors, especially within the body of Christ.

The next part of this verse says, "to which indeed you were called in one body," and this gives us the connection between the rule of peace and the fellowship of the members in the body of Christ, the Church. Maintaining unity within the body is a major reason for allowing peace to rule among the members. One commentator has said:

> It is a call to those who have been knit together in one body. All this confirms the view that it is the attitude of the believer to others which is still under consideration. Peace is to act as an umpire. The verb here translated rule would describe the activity of the umpire in the Olympic games who decides the contest. Thus in the inner conflict which would inevitably accompany many of their attitudes, when love and bitterness contend for mastery, peace is to be the governing factor. Membership in the one body of Christ involves a call to maintain peace among the members. Each member therefore must himself be governed by this inner desire for peace, and this peace is Christ's gift. [Carson, 89]

Finally, Paul adds his command for them to "be thankful." The commands in this verse are in the present tense, which means that believers are to continually do them and to make a habit of doing them. This last phrase could be translated, "Keep on becoming thankful." One commentator said, "A spirit of thankfulness would tend to promote harmony and peace. An ungrateful people is usually an agitated, restless, and dissatisfied people. Nothing better tends to promote peace and order than gratitude to God for his mercies." [Barnes]

In this verse when Paul adds "and be thankful" it almost seems like an afterthought, until we look at all three of the final verses in this section. As we will see shortly, Paul deliberately used "thankfulness" almost as an exclamation point at the end of each of these three verses. The idea of "thankfulness" is one of the main themes that appears throughout this letter. We see it mentioned seven times (Col 1:3, 12; 2:7; 3:15, 16, 17; 4:2), and so an attitude of thankfulness should permeate everything we do.

Col 3:16 - Let the word of Christ richly dwell within you, with all wisdom teaching and admonishing one another with psalms and hymns and spiritual songs, singing with thankfulness in your hearts to God.

"The word of Christ" appears at the beginning of the original sentence for emphasis. Here Paul is referring to the sum of all revelation that God gave, whether in the Old Testament, the words and work of Christ, or the new revelation – the mysteries – being given to the apostles and prophets in Paul's day for the Church Age. In our day today we have all of God's revelation together in one place, that is, in our Bible. When Paul speaks of God's revelation in his epistles, he typically uses the phrase "the word of God." Sometimes he adds other descriptive terms, such as "the word of faith, the word of the cross, the word of reconciliation, the word of truth, the word of the Lord, or the word of life." Across all of his epistles this is the only time Paul used "the word of Christ" but it makes perfect sense in this letter because he is emphasizing the greatness of Christ. Since the Lord Jesus Christ is God, here (instead of using his typical phrase "the word of God") Paul simply substitutes the equivalent word Christ for God. He is saying, "let the word of Christ, which is the word of God, richly dwell within you."

Paul's command is in the present tense, so he wants us to continually be in the habit of letting the word of God make its home within us. To **dwell within** is the Greek word *enoikeō* which has as its root the word *oikos* that is a house or dwelling place. So believers can think of themselves as the house where the word of God lives. **Richly** is a form of the same word Paul used in Col 1:27 where he said that "God willed to make known what is the riches of the glory of this mystery among the Gentiles." He also used this word in Col 2:2 where he said that believers should attain "all the wealth that comes from the full assurance of understanding, in a true knowledge of God's mystery." God's Word is our only source of true knowledge, which is something that Paul mentions throughout this letter. Just as he did in Col 2:3 where he said that "all the treasures of wisdom and knowledge" are hidden in Christ, here Paul also adds "with all wisdom." One commentator has said,

> Their experience of the word is not a merely individual one, for it is in the context of the fellowship of the Church that they are to learn its truths. Thus there must be a mutual sharing of the word of God. It is from the indwelling word that they will learn the wisdom of God, and that wisdom will then become the atmosphere in which they move as they seek to build one another up in knowledge. The worship of the Church is here viewed from the standpoint of the edification of the believers. [Carson, 90]

Now, in the last part of this verse there are three participles which have the same force as commands – teaching, admonishing, and singing – and they are all in the present tense, which means that believers should make a habit of doing them. The word of Christ is emphasized in this verse because it should be the foundation for accomplishing all of these things. **Teaching** (*didaskō*) involves giving instruction in the truths of the faith. **Admonishing** (*noutheteō*) literally means "to put in mind," and it involves calling attention to something, exhorting, or giving warnings." **Singing** (*adō*) means "to express praise and devotion to God through song," and Paul listed three types of songs: the psalms from the Old Testament, new hymns composed by Christians, and spiritual odes (literally) which might be chants, poems, or any words that are sung to express praise to God. But all singing must be grounded in the word of God as its foundation.

Earlier in chapter 1 Paul had described his own ministry which was given to him by God for the benefit of the Church. He said, "Of this church I was made a minister according to the stewardship from God bestowed on me for your benefit, so that I might fully carry out the preaching of the word of

God ... admonishing every man and teaching every man with all wisdom" (Col 1:25, 28). Paul had set the perfect example for the ministers who would come later. He was laser-focused on all the right things to benefit the body of Christ. One Bible commentator has this to say about the ministry of the word of God in the Christian fellowship:

> There is a danger today, as there was in Paul's day, that local churches minimize the Word of God. ... Many saved people cannot honestly say that God's Word dwells in their hearts richly, because they do not take time to read, study, and memorize it. ... If we do not know the Bible and understand it, we cannot honestly sing it from our hearts. [Wiersbe, 140]

Now, at the end of this verse Paul encourages thankfulness again. All of these activities in the body of Christ should be done in a spirit of gracious thanksgiving.

Col 3:17 - Whatever you do in word or deed, do all in the name of the Lord Jesus, giving thanks through Him to God the Father.

Here Paul is telling us, "Whatever you say or do," so this command covers all aspects of our behavior. The important truth here is that all of it must be done in the name of the Lord Jesus. There should be no compartmentalization in our lives between the secular and the sacred – between the spiritual and the worldly. Because believers are in Christ, everything is sacred and everything is spiritual.

To live in the name of the Lord Jesus means that we are representing Him in everything we do. We no longer live only for ourselves, but we live for Him and publicly represent Him and His standards. Our words and deeds must be chosen with a view to honoring Him, and our goal should be to bring Him glory. In order to do this, believers obviously must grow in their knowledge of Him and His ways. We must live in accordance with His pattern of life and in obedience to His authority. This is why it is so important that we "keep seeking the things above, where Christ is, seated at the right hand of God, setting our minds on the things above, not on the things that are on earth." (Col 3:1-2)

The name of the Lord Jesus sets what may seem like an impossibly high standard of living, so in order to please Him we must also rely on the help of the indwelling Holy Spirit. As Paul said in Col 1:27, it is only because of "Christ in you" that you have the "hope of glory." And if we are now living our lives in Christ, then it is through Him that our prayers, praise, and thanksgiving rise to God the Father. Living this way means that everything we do and say comes from a source which is "hidden with Christ in God" (Col 3:3), and that truly "Christ is all, and in all" (Col 3:11). Let us strive more and more to live our lives in the name and for the glory of the Lord Jesus Christ.

By way of application from these two chapters on the right ways to master the flesh, since believers are responsible for managing our thought life, are there things that you allow to dominate your thoughts, but which you know are not focused on the positive and gracious life which the Lord would want you to lead? When thoughts and ideas from your old nature rise to the surface, how are you dealing with them?

How is it going for you as you consider the members of your body to be dead to the sensual sins? Are there any relational sins that you tend to fall into? Old habits die hard, so look over the lists again to see if God brings specific attitudes or behaviors to mind which you need to deal with.

Do you have any preconceived notions or prejudices when it comes to social, racial, or class distinctions which Jesus says you are not to have? If so, what do you plan to do about them?

After putting off any of the negative attitudes and behaviors, what do you need to put on? Look over the list of positive qualities to see which ones you should make your highest priority.

Are you allowing the peace of Christ to rule your attitudes and actions when things become difficult? How would you rate yourself as a representative of the "name of the Lord Jesus?"

In Christ at Home

(Colossians 3:18-4:6)

So far in this letter to the Colossians Paul has shared some amazing truths about the greatness of Christ, which can be applied to believers' lives in order to help them to grow in spiritual maturity. In the last three chapters we spent time looking at Paul's explanation of how believers are to master their old nature, which Christians will continue to battle until we receive glorified bodies at the appearing of Christ for the Church. There are practices that believers are to avoid because they have no value against fleshly indulgence (Col 2:16-23), and there are also attitudes and behaviors that believers are to put off, as well as Christ-like character qualities which believers should put on (Col 3:1-17). All of these things will result in the renewal or transformation of believers as they grow in spiritual maturity, living in ways which please, honor, and glorify Christ.

Many of these new character traits will be publicly apparent to others, but it's also possible that others, even within the body of Christ, the Church, may not notice some of the more private attitudes and behaviors. There is one place, however, where it is very difficult to hide any aspect of one's character, and that place is within one's family and household. Those relationships are much more intimate and constant, so a person's true character will be more visible at home. This is the arena which Paul now moves into, as he provides even more guidance for specific household relationships.

Col 3:18 - Wives, be subject to your husbands, as is fitting in the Lord.

Paul begins by speaking to the Christian wives, but his starting with them does not indicate anything in the way of priority, either negatively or positively. This is simply the way Paul typically begins in all of his epistles. He almost always starts by addressing those who are under authority before addressing those who will bear ultimate responsibility.

Here in Colossians Paul does not specifically say that it is the husband who will ultimately give an account to God for the welfare of his wife and household. But in the more detailed parallel passage in his letter to the Ephesians he says, "For the husband is the head of the wife, as Christ also is the head of the church." (Eph 5:23) This was God's choice and design from the beginning, even though we may not fully comprehend the reasons for such an arrangement of accountability. In another of Paul's letters he described God's structure of responsibility this way: "But I want you to understand that Christ is the head of every man, and the man is the head of a woman, and God is the head of Christ" (1 Cor 11:3). This verse outlines a hierarchy of responsibility: God, then Christ, then the husband, then the wife. Jesus is the best example of someone who is under proper authority, and it may have been listed last in 1 Cor 11:3 for emphasis. It is also possible that Paul put it last to encourage wives that when they are properly in relationship, they are like their Lord who is also under proper authority. The spiritual equality of men and women before the Lord (Gal 3:28), however, is still fully in effect. One commentator has this to say about these relationships within God's structure of responsibility:

> It should be understood clearly that the term head and its corresponding opposite, subjection, have to do with rank, position, and authority; not at all with ability. They denote positions in governmental or administrative organization. They do not in any way reflect inferiority or inequality. Proof of this is seen in the

relationships within the Godhead. Christ is every bit as much God as God the Father. He is equal in essence. But, He is second in the Godhead and subordinate to the Father in function (John 4:34; 5:18-19). In another realm, an army captain may not be a better man, either physically or intellectually or morally, than the private. But he is superior in rank and function. So the Christian wife, even though she may be superior to her husband in ability, in personality, even in spirituality, yet she recognizes his headship and gets in rank under him in the divine economy of the home. [Boyer, 104]

So, here in Col 3:18 Paul says wives are to be **subject** to their husbands. This is the Greek word *hupotassō* which literally means "to arrange under." It is a military term that means "to be under in rank," and describes the way that an army is organized by levels of rank. The middle voice of this verb indicates that their subjection is voluntary.

A wife doesn't submit to her husband because he deserves it, but because God has put him in a position of responsibility and accountability for the wife and the household. In a sense, the wife becomes the gifted support system which makes it possible for the husband to give a good report to his superior for the state of the entire household.

It is important to note that at the end of this verse Paul added, "as is fitting in the Lord." **Fitting** is the Greek word *anēkō* which literally means "to come up to." It is often translated as something that is fitting, proper, appropriate, or suitable. It is befitting the condition of being in Christ. So Paul is saying that it is only fitting or proper that a Christian wife would recognize and honor God's design for household accountability.

The apostle Peter said that even if a Christian wife is married to an unbelieving or disobedient husband, her obedience to the Lord's structure of responsibility can have a powerful influence on a husband even though he may not be following the Lord. He said, "In the same way, you wives, be submissive to your own husbands so that even if any of them are disobedient to the word, they may be won without a word by the behavior of their wives" (1 Peter 3:1).

We do need to recognize the wise advice of Acts 5:29, which says, "We must obey God rather than man." This provides some boundaries for all human authority. For example, if the husband tells the wife to sin, she must recognize that ultimately she and her husband are both under a higher authority whose standards must be obeyed.

When a wife is following God's design and is properly "in rank" with her husband, she has a position of tremendous influence in his life. She has the ability to properly appeal to her husband to change direction and to obey God (see the book of Esther for a biblical example).

Col 3:19 - Husbands, love your wives and do not be embittered against them.

Paul now addresses Christian husbands. Husbands must also recognize the God-given structure of responsibility which puts them *hupotassō* or "under in rank." As it says in Rom 13:1, all authority comes from God, and all those in authority are accountable to God for rightly fulfilling their responsibilities. Ultimately every individual must answer to God for his thoughts, words, and deeds, but the one in authority will be judged more strictly. As the principle is stated in Luke 12:48, "From everyone who has been given much, much will be required; and to whom they entrusted much, of him they will ask all the more." This humbling truth should provide greater motivation for Christian husbands to do what Paul commands them to do.

Paul now gives husbands two commands. First, the husband is to **love** (*agapaō*) his wife. As we have seen throughout this letter, *agape* love is the highest form of love – God's kind of love – and it is almost impossible for a person to display this type of love without the help of the indwelling Holy Spirit. But this command is in the present tense, so it means that the husband is to be in the habit of continually loving his wife this way. As we have seen before, *agape* love is unselfish and giving, or even self-sacrificing to the point of "giving up" things for someone else. It is the kind of love that always has the other person's best interests at heart. As one commentator said,

> The word has little to do with emotion; it has much to do with self-denial for the sake of another. We can read this passage and think that Paul means, "Husband, be kind to your wife." Or "Husband, be nice to your wife." There is no doubt that for many marriages, this would be a huge improvement. But that isn't what Paul writes about. What he really means is, "Husband, continually practice self-denial for the sake of your wife." [Guzik]

So, Paul now adds, "and do not be embittered against them." **Embittered** is the Greek word *pikrainō* which means "exasperated to the point of irritation." This verb is a present imperative, which could be translated "do not have the habit of being bitter." As one commentator said,

> The implication is that perhaps the wife has given the husband some reason to be bitter. Paul says, "That doesn't matter, husband." The husband may feel perfectly justified in his harsh or unloving attitude and actions towards his wife, but he is not justified – no matter how the wife has behaved towards the husband. [Guzik]

What we saw in the previous chapters can be applied to husbands here. When something difficult occurs which provokes a response, Christian husbands are to "put off anger, wrath, malice, slander, and abusive speech" and they are to "put on kindness, humility, gentleness, patience, forbearance, and forgiveness." And, just as we saw previously, over all of these qualities the husband is to put on *agape* love for his wife. This kind of servant-hearted self-sacrificing love would go a long way toward making it easier for the wife to obey the Lord in her role in God's structure of responsibility. Because the husband and wife live in such closeness, opportunities for friction will be inevitable. The marriage relationship will probably be the first place that differences and difficulties may appear in all our relationships with others. So the husband-wife relationship will be the most obvious and important place for believers to put Paul's words into practice, as we have already seen in the last few sections of this letter to the Colossians.

Now Paul continues his pattern of addressing those under authority before speaking to the ones in authority.

Col 3:20 - Children, be obedient to your parents in all things, for this is well-pleasing to the Lord.

To Christian children he says, "be obedient to your parents." The word **obedient** is the Greek word *hupakouō* which literally means "to listen under." It carries the idea of paying attention and choosing to respect and submit to the wishes of the parents. We should remember that Paul is speaking to believers here, so these are children who have reached the age of accountability and have placed their faith in Christ for their salvation. All children should be taught to do this, but here Paul commands believing children to listen, respect, and follow the wishes of their parents.

This command obviously applies to the children who are living in their parent's household. Once children have grown to adulthood and have left to start families of their own, this command no longer applies in the same way. As adult children, they have the responsibility to honor their parents and to give consideration to their advice and counsel. As one commentator has said, "When a child is grown and out of his parents' household, he is no longer under the same obligation of obedience, but the obligation to honor your father and mother remains." [Guzik]

For Christian children, Jesus provides the perfect example to follow. When He was twelve years old He went to Jerusalem with His family for the Feast of Passover. But when His family left for home, Jesus remained to speak with the teachers in the temple. His parents searched anxiously for Him in Jerusalem and finally found Him. It seemed natural for Jesus to be in His Father's house, but He saw how He had worried His parents. Luke 2:51 gives His response: "And He went down with them and came to Nazareth, and He continued in subjection to them; and His mother treasured all these things in her heart."

At the end of this verse Paul gives the reason for Christian children to be obedient to their parents. He says "for this is well-pleasing to the Lord." Children who have put their faith in Christ for their salvation are not only growing in physical, mental, and social stature, but they are on the road to spiritual maturity as well. Even children can "walk in a manner worthy of the Lord, to please Him in all respects" (Col 1:10).

Col 3:21 - Fathers, do not exasperate your children, so that they will not lose heart.

Now, on the other side of the coin, fathers – and really both parents – have a responsibility to treat their children well. The word **exasperate** is the Greek word *erethizō* which means "to stir up, provoke, or irritate." This verb is a present imperative, so Paul is saying that fathers are not to be in the habit of continually exasperating their children. One commentator explained this in the following words: "Parents, and especially fathers, are urged not to irritate their children by being so unreasonable in their demands that their children lose heart and come to think that it is useless trying to please their parents." [Guzik]

At the end of this verse Paul shared the inevitable consequences if fathers continue to treat them poorly. He says that they will lose heart. To **lose heart** is the Greek word *athymeō* which literally means "without passion" and by implication, discouraged to the point of hopelessness.

As one commentator has said, children who are exasperated "will not feel the love and the support from their parents like they should, and they will come to believe that the whole world is against them because they feel their parents are against them. This reminds us how important it is to season our parenting with lots of grace. We should be as gracious, gentle, forgiving, and longsuffering with our children as God is with us." [Guzik]

Since God has entrusted these young precious souls to our care, it becomes that much more important to treat them well by "putting off anger, wrath, malice, slander, and abusive speech" and by "putting on kindness, humility, gentleness, patience, forbearance, and forgiveness." And of course, over all of these to put on love. Christian fathers are no longer bound to follow ungodly or worldly patterns of child raising – they are not fettered to their past or to societal norms which run contrary to God's ways. Believers can "keep seeking the things above, where Christ is" (Col 3:1), and we can follow Christ's example in all things, including His instructions for Christian parenting.

Col 3:22 - Slaves, in all things obey those who are your masters on earth, not with external service, as those who merely please men, but with sincerity of heart, fearing the Lord.

Paul now turns his attention to those who are Christian servants within the household. The word translated here as "**slaves**" is the Greek word *doulos* which is commonly translated as "servant" or "bondservant." In our day today, the topic of slaves and masters is considered anathema, and even using these words is discouraged or condemned. In Paul's day, however, being a servant under someone else's authority was the norm. One commentator has said that, "More than half the people seen on the streets of the great cities of the Roman world were slaves. And this was the status of the majority of 'professional' people such as teachers and doctors as well as that of menials and craftsmen." [Guzik] Paul is using an aspect of daily life in New Testament times to communicate a truth about how those under authority are to relate to those in authority over them, especially within a Christian household.

The Greek word *doulos* is the same word that Paul used in his epistles at least thirty times to refer to himself, his fellow ministers, or other believers generally as the slaves of Christ. Paul even used this concept to communicate an important truth about the incarnation of Christ when he said, in Phil 2:7, that Christ "emptied Himself, taking the form of a bond-servant, being made in the likeness of men." So we can think of this term as being used generally to speak about relationships with those in positions of authority who are responsible for us.

So far in this passage we have seen Paul devote one verse each to wives, then husbands, to children, then parents. But now instead of following that pattern and devoting one verse to servants, Paul writes four verses to servants before addressing masters in a single verse. Why did Paul use four times as many verses addressing servants? One commentator said: "It will be noted that this section is far longer than the others; and its length may well be due to long talks which Paul had with the runaway slave, Onesimus, whom later he was to send back to his master Philemon." [Guzik] We will meet Onesimus in the final section of this letter, but for now we can assume that Paul learned quite a bit from him about the way servants typically behaved. This may have given Paul new insights which he used to correct that behavior for servants who are believers in Christ.

He begins by saying "in all things obey those who are your masters on earth." As we mentioned before, there are limits to all human authority. When someone in a position of authority tells a believer who is under authority to sin, then the believer must acknowledge the higher authority of God whose standards must be obeyed, rather than the sinful wishes of men. As Paul said in the previous section, a believer must do everything in the name of the Lord Jesus, because he graciously and humbly represents his heavenly Master. But in the normal course of daily life as someone in service to others, believers are to obey those in authority.

The word **obey** is the Greek word *hupakouō*, which is the same word that was used for the obedience of children in verse 20. As it did there, here it means to pay close attention and choose to respect and submit to the wishes of the one in authority. The words "masters on earth" could be translated literally as "lords according to the flesh." This is Paul's way of referring to our earthly authorities, and it stands in direct contrast to a believer's "Master in heaven."

Paul ends this verse with a negative example of behavior, followed immediately by a positive example of behavior for a believer who serves. First he says, "not with external service, as those who merely please men." **External service** is the single Greek word *ophthalmodouleia* which literally means "eye-service" or service that is given only while under the watchful eye of the one in authority. I'm sure that all of us can think of times when we ourselves or others we know have done this. We try to look busy when the boss is around, but as soon as he is gone we take a deep breath and slow down or completely slack off in the work. This is the kind of work attitude that attempts to "merely please men" as Paul says here. It means only doing the minimum amount of labor to just get by while the boss is watching.

But we might ask this person, "Where is your pride in your work and your sense of personal accomplishment? Isn't that important to you?" At the end of this verse Paul is basically saying the same thing. Instead of a worker behaving like he just described, he says believers should work "with sincerity of heart, fearing the Lord." They should put their heart into their work as a matter of personal integrity. The word translated **sincerity** is the Greek word *haplotēs* which literally means "singleness" or singleness of purpose. This contrasts with the negative example Paul presented of a worker who is two-faced or deceitful in working only when under supervision. One of the reasons why believers should work this way is because they have a Master or supervisor who is always watching. As Paul says here, believers should "fear the Lord," which means that they will be constantly aware of His presence and desire to reverence, honor, and obey Him no matter what their "lords according to the flesh" might say or do.

What Paul has said here to household servants is important and powerful in itself, but he goes on in the next three verses to elaborate on what he means.

Col 3:23-24 - Whatever you do, do your work heartily, as for the Lord rather than for men, knowing that from the Lord you will receive the reward of the inheritance. It is the Lord Christ whom you serve.

Paul had already said in Col 3:17 that "Whatever you do in word or deed, do all in the name of the Lord Jesus." But here he is specifically speaking to workers under the authority of men. He says, "whatever you do" – in whatever field or occupation they are serving – they are to "work heartily." In the last verse Paul had said they were to work with sincerity of heart and there he used the Greek word *kardia*, which is the heart. Here, though, he used the Greek word *psuchē* which is the soul. Paul is saying that believers are to put their very soul into their work, because they know they are working for the Lord rather than for men. This attitude toward work is really a simple matter of understanding who your real boss is. Since believers are trying to live lives that please the Lord, then this will apply to everything they do, including their work or service to others.

Here in Col 3:24 Paul goes on to explain that this involves a little more than knowing who your real boss is. It also involves knowing that from the Lord you will receive the reward. This means that believers understand who is really giving them their paycheck. But much more is at stake than their earthly wages – it extends to their heavenly reward. Believers understand that our "momentary, light affliction is producing for us an eternal weight of glory far beyond all comparison" (2 Cor 4:17). Paul is referring to "the inheritance of the saints in Light" which he mentioned in Col 1:12. They will be given a portion of the property and privileges waiting for believers in heaven for eternity.

If there were any doubt, Paul now states it simply and clearly: "It is the Lord Christ whom you serve." Believers are bondservants of Christ in subjection to His Lordship, and Christ's standards of behavior and workmanship are what believers must attain to. In seeking to please Christ, they will certainly exceed the standards of their earthly authorities, not only with the quality of their work but with the quality of their whole lives.

Col 3:25 - For he who does wrong will receive the consequences of the wrong which he has done, and that without partiality.

Here Paul states a general principle, but he specifically applies it to believers who are serving under earthly authorities. It is possible that Paul may have learned from Onesimus that the behavior of servants he described in the last three verses was so common that it required a specific warning to servants. **Wrong** is the Greek word *adikeō* which comes from the root word *dikē*, meaning right or just. So *adikeō* means to be unrighteous or unjust, to actively do wrong (morally, socially or physically), to hurt or injure, to be an offender.

This verse in the original language contains only ten words. A literal translation might be, "For the wrongdoer will be repaid the wrong, and without partiality." The phrase "will receive the consequences" translates the single Greek word *komizō* which means "to receive back." This is the same word Paul used in his earlier letter to the church in Corinth when he said, "For we must all appear before the judgment seat of Christ, so that each one may be recompensed for his deeds in the body" (2 Cor 5:10). Whether in this life or the next, wrongdoers will suffer the consequences for their wrongs.

The next phrase, **of the wrong which he has done**, translates the word *adikeō*, which is the same word he used in the first part of this verse for being unjust or doing wrong. The one doing wrong will suffer the consequences for his wrong. One commentator has said, "It was possible for an unfaithful servant to wrong and defraud his master in a great variety of ways without being detected; but let them remember what is said here: God sees him, and will punish him for his breach of honesty and trust." [Guzik]

The phrase **there is no partiality** translates the Greek word *prosōpolēpsia* which literally means "to accept the face." People tend to make judgments about others based on external qualities which they can see on the outside. This word describes someone who is a respecter of persons; someone who displays partiality or favoritism. But this is not true of God who sees all and knows all, both inside and out. Rom 2:11 declares, "For there is no partiality with God." One commentator summarized the message of this verse:

> For ancient Christian slaves and for modern Christian workers, there is no guarantee on earth of fair treatment from those whom they work for. Sometimes partiality means that bad workers are unfairly rewarded and good employees are penalized or left unrewarded. Paul assures both our ancient brethren and us that there is a final reward and punishment, and with this there is no partiality. [Guzik]

Col 4:1 - Masters, grant to your slaves justice and fairness, knowing that you too have a Master in heaven.

Now Paul turns from addressing the servants to addressing their "masters on earth" (Col 3:22). They are to grant justice and fairness. **Justice** is the Greek word *dikaios* that is a positive form of the word *adikeō*, which meant the opposite of justice and righteousness. Even if a servant were to do wrong or behave unjustly, Paul commands the household master to grant justice. **Fairness** is the Greek word *isotēs* which means equity or having equal proportions. It means they are to provide no less than what is due. One commentator has said this about the implications of Paul's words here:

> How astonished Roman lawgivers would have been if they could have heard Paul talking about justice and equity as applied to a slave! What a strange new dialect it must have sounded to the slave owners in the Colossian Church! They would not see how far the principle, thus quietly introduced, was to carry succeeding ages; they could not dream of the great tree that was to spring from this tiny seed precept. [Expositors]

The reason Paul gives for masters to grant justice and equity is almost identical to the motivation he gave to the servants. Here he says, "you too have a Master in heaven." As one commentator said, "You have a Master in heaven is the great principle on which all Christian duty rests. Christ's command is our law, His will is supreme, His authority is absolute, His example all-sufficient." [Expositors]

Paul will now share some instructions about the Colossians' prayer life before he mentions their relationship with outsiders.

Col 4:2 - Devote yourselves to prayer, keeping alert in it with an attitude of thanksgiving;

In the original Greek sentence the word **prayer** occurs first for emphasis. Paul could have used the Greek verb *proseuchomai* in the present tense to say "keep on praying." Instead he uses the noun for prayer (*proseuchē*), and then follows it with a powerful verb. This is the Greek word *proskartereō* which literally means "to be strong toward" something. It carries the idea of persisting in adherence to a thing; to be intently engaged in something, and to attend constantly to something. This is an imperative or command in the present tense, which emphasizes how constantly they are to engage in prayer. It sounds redundant to state it this way, but we could paraphrase this as, "continually be in the habit of persisting in prayer."

When he says "**keeping alert** in it" he used the Greek word *grēgoreō* which means to stay awake or be vigilant. While it certainly is important to stay awake during times of prayer (see Matt 26:36-46), believers should keep alert for opportunities to bring things before their Lord throughout their day. When something happens or when you learn about a new situation, is prayer your first thought? We should become more and more alert to opportunities to pray about all of the things we encounter in our lives.

With an attitude of thanksgiving is literally "in thanksgiving." Once again Paul encourages a spirit of thankfulness, this time as part of a believer's prayer life. As was mentioned in a previous chapter, thankfulness is one of the main themes that appears throughout this letter. We see it mentioned seven times (Col 1:3, 12; 2:7; 3:15, 16, 17; 4:2), so an attitude of thankfulness should permeate everything we do.

One commentator suggested that there may be three stages of prayer illustrated here. He said, "The connection here with thanksgiving may suggest the threefold rhythm: intercession, watching for answers to prayer, and thanksgiving when answers appear." [Guzik]

Col 4:3 - praying at the same time for us as well, that God will open up to us a door for the word, so that we may speak forth the mystery of Christ, for which I have also been imprisoned;

Now, as the first word in this verse Paul does use the Greek word *proseuchomai* which was mentioned previously. It is in the present tense which means "keep on praying," and this is the same word Paul used in Col 1:2 and 9 when he said that he was constantly praying for them. Now he is asking them to pray for him and his ministry team whenever they are in prayer. Paul gives them two prayer requests.

First, he asks them to pray that God will "open up a door" so he can preach the word. This is a metaphor that was used several other times (Act 14:27; 1 Cor 16:9; 2 Cor 2:12) and he is asking that God would create an opportunity for him to speak the word of the gospel. He specifically identifies this word as the mystery of Christ. We know from how Paul previously used the term **mystery** (*mustērion*) in this letter that he is referring to the new revelation God had given to the New Testament apostles and prophets for the Church Age. Paul then adds that proclaiming this mystery is the reason he has been imprisoned for so long.

If we look at the last eight chapters of the book of Acts we will see the series of events for which he had been imprisoned (Acts 21 - 28). It had been a long and difficult time of confinement for Paul. But the exact words he was speaking which resulted in his imprisonment are recorded in Acts 22:1-21. Paul had been sharing his personal testimony about what happened to him on the road to Damascus where the Lord Jesus confronted him and he came to faith in Christ. Then Paul shared these words which Jesus Himself had spoken to him: "And He said to me, 'Go! For I will send you far away to the Gentiles'" (Acts 22:21). The next verse, Acts 22:22, says, "They listened to him up to this statement, and then they raised their voices and said, 'Away with such a fellow from the earth, for he should not be allowed to live!'" Those Jews in Jerusalem were reacting against the words of Christ which revealed a previously unrevealed mystery – that God had opened the door for the Gentiles to be included in the new entity called the body of Christ, the Church, on the same basis as Jews. Jews and Gentiles alike would now be accepted by God on an equal basis, with the only requirement being faith in what Christ accomplished when He paid the ransom price on the cross to redeem the whole world. This is why Paul was imprisoned, and he asks for prayer that God might give him more opportunities like that.

Col 4:4 - that I may make it clear in the way I ought to speak.

Paul's second prayer request was for guidance in exactly how he should present the word of the gospel so that it would have the greatest effect. He wants to "**make it clear.**" This is the Greek word *phaneroō* which literally means "to bring something into the light." It has the idea of making something visible, making it apparent or making it known, as well as making it clearly and thoroughly understood. Paul wants to be a better communicator.

In the phrase "the way I ought to speak" the word translated **ought** is the little Greek word *dei*. It conveys the idea of a necessity or a binding obligation, and in this case it means "exactly what is needed in order to accomplish a specific goal." That goal is the salvation and eternal destiny of the individuals to whom Paul is given the opportunity to speak. Each individual might require or need to hear something tailored specifically to his level of understanding in order to respond to the word of the gospel. This may be something that only God can give insight into at exactly the right time and place in a person's life, so Paul is requesting prayer that God would give him what is needed at just the right moment.

Col 4:5 - Conduct yourselves with wisdom toward outsiders, making the most of the opportunity.

Now Paul turns his attention to the Colossians and how they should behave toward those who are outside the Christian family and the Church family. The words **conduct yourselves** is actually the single Greek word *peripateō* which, as we have seen previously, literally means "to walk about" and was commonly used as a metaphor for all aspects of a person's lifestyle. In Col 1:10 Paul told them he was praying that they might "walk in a manner worthy of the Lord." Then in Col 2:6 he said that, "as you have received Christ Jesus the Lord, so walk in Him." Now in Col 4:5 he commands them to live and behave wisely before the watching world. One commentator expressed it this way:

> Presumably, these believers are a minority in their community. They have no church building. They have no New Testament. They are without gospel tracts. How are they going to commend the gospel? Paul points to their walk, their daily conduct in the sight of their fellows. He is saying that their conduct can have a powerful evangelizing influence on the unsaved; for, if these people see a type of life that is superior to their own, the chances are good that they will want to inquire after its secret. This will lead to conversation about Christ and His saving work. [Harrison, 105-106]

At the end of this verse Paul says, "making the most of every opportunity." Literally he says, "buying up the time." This phrase is unique to the apostle Paul (see Eph 5:16) and he adds it here because he wants us to be aware that our time is short, so we should make the most of it. He doesn't want us to waste a single moment behaving in a silly or sinful way that might ruin our testimony to those who are watching.

Col 4:6 - Let your speech always be with grace, as though seasoned with salt, so that you will know how you should respond to each person.

One large part of our lifestyle and behavior involves how we speak to others, so Paul will finish this section by explaining how we are to talk with those around us. He literally says, "the words of you always in grace." There is no verb, but the meaning is clear. Whatever we say must measure up to the standard of **grace** (*charis*), which is defined as "that which affords joy, pleasure, delight, sweetness, charm, loveliness, good will, loving-kindness, and favor."

Paul then adds that our words should be "seasoned with salt" which may seem like an obscure way to explain what he means. This expression is not used by other New Testament writers, so it seems unique to the apostle Paul. He is saying that, just like seasoning adds flavor to food and makes it more pleasant to eat, we should choose our words carefully so that they become more pleasant and agreeable to those who are listening. It is possible that Paul included this figure of speech here because of the report of an ancient salt deposit near Colossae which supplied the surrounding area with salt. [Herodotus] In any case, Paul commands believers to eliminate any coarse, crude, or unpleasant words from our conversation with those who are outside the family of God.

Paul ends this verse by giving the reason why believers must carefully watch their words. He says, "so that you will know how you should respond to each person." This phrase is very similar to what Paul asked the Colossians to pray for himself and his ministry partners in Col 4:4. In that verse he asked for prayer to know exactly what to say so each individual would hear the words they require or need to hear, so they could respond to the gospel. Now in this verse he uses the same Greek word (*dei*) again. Here it is translated "**should**," but it expresses the same idea. For **each person** *(heis hekastos)* – each and every single one – we are obligated to share words tailored to their situation and their level of understanding. If our speech is gracious and appealing, then God will allow us to see exactly what is needed to respond to whoever we are speaking with.

This is a tall order for all of us, since the tongue is so difficult to control in the best of circumstances. But just as we have the indwelling Holy Spirit to help us put off sinful attitudes and behaviors while putting on Christ-like qualities, He will also provide the insight that we need in order to speak with those outside the family of God in a winsome way.

When we think of applying the truths in this chapter, it will be a matter of looking down the list of verses for the role or roles that you fulfill. For example, some of you may be husbands, fathers, and employees – so there are three passages that apply to you. Husbands, don't go to the passage about wives or children and start pointing fingers or laying blame. Saying "you didn't" or "you never" can damage a relationship.

– Wives, are you in proper rank?
– Husbands, are you sacrificially loving?
– Children, are you obeying?
– Parents, are you disheartening your children?
– Servers, are you putting your soul into your work?
– Leaders, are you granting justice and fairness?

How would you rate the consistency and alertness of your prayer life? When things arise during your day, are you bringing them to the Lord first? Which of your spiritual leaders do you need to add to your regular prayer times?

What do you think you should change in your behavior, especially toward unbelievers that you regularly come in contact with? How would you rate the graciousness and pleasantness of your manner of speaking? Is there someone for whom you need wisdom in how to respond to meet their needs?

Let's ask God for His help as we seek to be more Christ-like toward others around us.

Paul's Companions

(Colossians 4:7-18)

As we have studied the book of Colossians, we have followed the apostle Paul's flow of thought from the beginning, and here in this final passage we will see Paul change the subject to include personal greetings from several of his trusted companions.

Col 4:7 - As to all my affairs, Tychicus, our beloved brother and faithful servant and fellow bond-servant in the Lord, will bring you information.

Paul now turns to more personal matters. There are things he wants to share with the Colossians, but the Holy Spirit led him not to record them in print. Beyond what he wrote to the Colossians, he also wants his faithful messenger Tychicus to spend time sharing additional information with them personally.

This is the first time that we hear of **Tychicus** in this letter, even though he was the messenger who delivered it to the church there. From other Bible passages we learn that Tychicus had been one of Paul's companions and part of his ministry team for several years before Paul's imprisonment in Rome. For example, we know that Tychicus was one of the trusted messengers who helped Paul to carry the funds that had been collected for the relief effort to the church in Judea (Acts 20:4). He was a man of proven character even at that time, which was probably as much as five years earlier than the writing of Colossians. And we know that Tychicus would continue to serve with Paul in ministry up until the time of

Paul's death about four or five years in the future from the time of Colossians (Titus 3:12; 2 Tim 4:12).

Even though we don't know very much about Tychicus, Paul's brief description of him here in Col 4:7 is a fitting tribute. Paul provided three important statements about the character of Tychicus:

Beloved brother is the Greek phrase *agapētos adelphos*. This is Paul's way of saying that Tychicus is very dear and precious to him, as well as clearly identifying Tychicus as a fellow-believer or brother in Christ. As one lexicon puts it, Paul and Tychicus were "joined in the bonds of faith and love." So the first of Paul's statements is that Tychicus is extremely important to Paul personally, as well as being a trusted ministry partner.

Faithful servant is the Greek phrase *pistos diakonos*. The noun *diakonos* is where we get our English word "deacon" which is one of the biblical offices recognized in the New Testament church (1 Tim 3:8), and it is often translated as "minister." The adjective *pistos* indicates that not only was Tychicus a believer, but he is faithful in the sense of being reliable, dependable, and trustworthy. *pistos diakonos* could mean, "Paul's trusted assistant." In the context we can conclude that Paul is authorizing Tychicus as his official representative for sharing the personal parts of his message to the church at Colossae.

Fellow bondservant is the single Greek word *sundoulos*, which means "one who serves under the same conditions as another; a servant of the same Lord." Here Paul is describing the bond of fellowship that he shares with Tychicus in their dedicated service to Christ and His body, the Church.

This gives us a glimpse into Paul's relationship with Tychicus, as well as endorsing him and his mission to the Colossians. Paul says that Tychicus will **bring you information** which translates the Greek word *gnōrizō* that means "to declare or make known."

Col 4:8 - For I have sent him to you for this very purpose, that you may know about our circumstances and that he may encourage your hearts;

There are two main purposes for Tychicus' visit to Colossae. First, he wants Tychicus to share about the circumstances and events that Paul has experienced in Rome. The reason for Paul's imprisonment was common knowledge throughout the Church, and the believers would need to be updated about the status of his case that was pending before Caesar. Paul's physical health had also been a constant concern during all of his missionary journeys across the region, so people would want to know how best to pray for his health issues. Pending the outcome of his case, people would want to know more about Paul's plans for continuing his work. It seems that Paul was ever the optimist, and he asked one member of the Colossian church to prepare a guest room for him so he could visit Colossae after his expected release from confinement (Philemon 1:22).

Second, Tychicus is a faithful minister who is well qualified to encourage the church members in Colossae. **Encourage** is the Greek word *parakaleō* which means "to call alongside to encourage, strengthen, and comfort." The **heart** is Paul's way to identify the center of a person's physical and spiritual life. As we have seen Paul say throughout this letter, the primary way that believers are encouraged and strengthened is from the ministry of the word of God (Col 1:9, 25-29; 2:2-3; 3:16). Tychicus was fully qualified to carry out that ministry, as we can see from later passages when Paul dispatched him to relieve other ministers. In one case he was sent to Crete to free up Titus (Titus 3:12) and on another occasion Paul sent him to Ephesus, possibly to relieve Timothy (2 Tim 4:12).

So Tychicus was commissioned on a special journey from Rome to Colossae. One commentator had this to say about Tychicus and his mission:

> Fleeting things done for Christ are eternal. How astonished Tychicus would have been if anybody had told him on that day when he got away from Rome, with the precious letters in his bag, that these bits of parchment would outlast all the ostentatious pomp of the city, and that his name, because it was written in them, would be known to the end of time all over the world! [Expositors]

Let's take a moment to figure out how Paul's letters traveled from Rome to Colossae. In Paul's day it was quite a bit more difficult to deliver letters than it is today. The Roman Empire did have an official postal service, and their system of roads connected all of the far-flung points across the entire empire. Their messenger service was called the *cursus publicus* and it was a state-controlled courier system. The Roman historian Procopius wrote: "The earlier emperors established couriers throughout their dominion. At a day's journey for an active man they fixed stages, and in every stage there were forty horses and a number of grooms in proportion. The couriers often covered in a single day as great a distance as they would otherwise have covered in ten." This sounds simi-

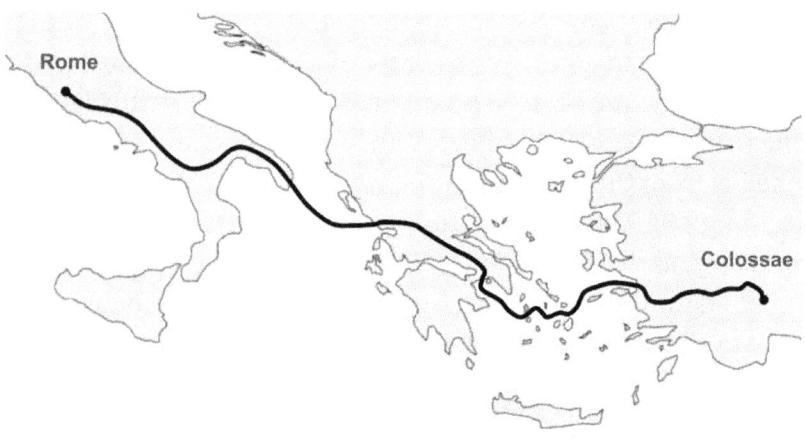

Route map: Rome to Colossae

lar to the Pony Express system that existed for a short time across the American West. Unfortunately, the *cursus publicus* was for official use only, and citizens were not allowed to use it without a special government permit. Normal citizens without access to the *cursus publicus* would have slaves or acquaintances carry their mail from place to place.

The trip from Rome to Colossae began with a journey of almost 400 miles from Rome to one of the ports in southeastern Italy. Next there was a journey across the Ionian Sea of over 100 miles. Then there was a journey of about 200 miles by land to one of the ports in southeastern Greece. Next was another 200 mile journey across the Aegean Sea to the port of Ephesus or Miletus on the western coast of Asia Minor. Finally, there was a journey by land of about 100 miles to reach Colossae.

Another interesting view of the route between Rome and Colossae is shown on the Tabula Peutingeriana. This is thought to be the only surviving map of the Roman *cursus publicus*. The map consists of an enormous scroll measuring over 22 feet long. It is a schematic map, similar to a modern subway map. Along the entire width of the scroll it displays the Roman routes and destinations. Any geographical features appear distorted and out of proportion, but the waypoints and distances between stages are accurately represented. Here we see just two small segments from the scroll, one at the starting point in Rome and the other near the destination in Asia Minor.

So Tychicus was dispatched to Colossae carrying these precious letters from the apostle Paul to the churches. One reason for selecting him as the messenger may have been that he was a native of Asia Minor, probably of Ephesus, so he would have known the territory and been acquainted with people along the way who could assist him during the journey.

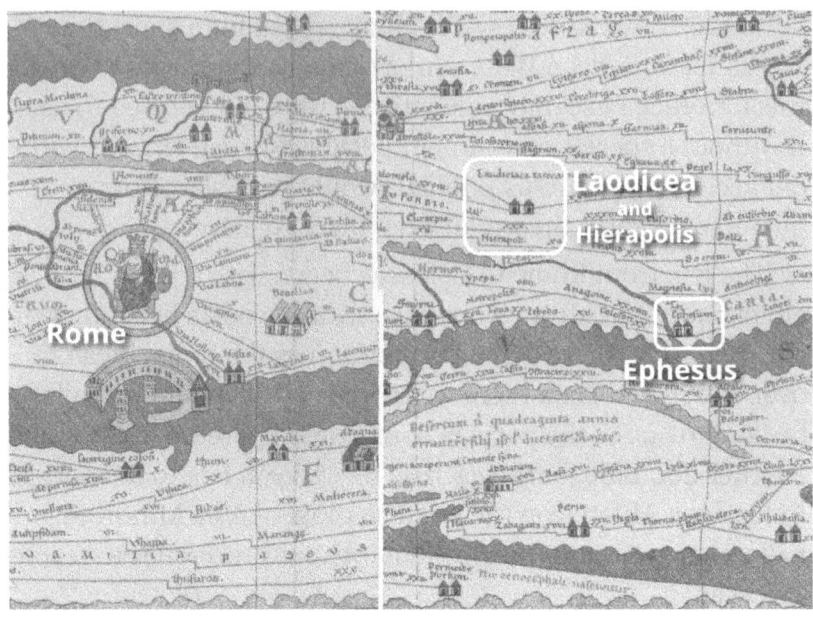

Route map: Tabula Peutingeriana (excerpts)

Col 4:9 - and with him Onesimus, our faithful and beloved brother, who is one of your number. They will inform you about the whole situation here.

So, Tychicus did not travel alone. He was accompanied by Onesimus, who was a runaway slave from the household of Philemon. We know very little about Onesimus himself or what motivated him to flee from his master's house. We do know that Philemon was a committed believer and that a church was meeting in his house at Colossae (Philemon 1:1-2). So Onesimus left that Christian environment and ran away. Rome was a huge city at that time, offering plenty of places to hide for someone who did not want to be found. But most of the best areas for hiding were also quite dangerous, with many opportunities to be taken advantage of.

We can only speculate about what brought Onesimus and Paul together in Rome. One commentator said, "What brought him into contact with Paul we do not know. It may have been hunger; it may have been the pangs of conscience. He could not forget that his master's house in Colossae was the place where the Christians met in their weekly assemblies for the worship of Christ. Neither could he forget how Philemon had many a time spoken of Paul, to whom he owed his conversion." [ISBE] The problem with running away from God is that wherever you go, there He is.

However it happened, we can be sure that God was looking out for Onesimus and that He led both Onesimus and Paul to meet each other in Rome. Paul explained to Philemon that while he was confined under house arrest, he met and ministered to Onesimus who became a Christian. Paul said it this way: "I appeal to you for my child Onesimus, whom I have begotten in my imprisonment, who formerly was useless to you, but now is useful both to you and to me. I have sent him back to you in person, that is, sending my very heart, whom I wished to keep with me, so that on your behalf he might minister to me in my imprisonment for the gospel; but without your consent I did not want to do anything, so that your goodness would not be, in effect, by compulsion but of your own free will." (Philemon 1:10-14)

So when Paul sent Tychicus to Colossae with his letter to that church, it seemed like the perfect opportunity to send Onesimus back to Philemon too. Paul could have written something like this: "I am sending Onesimus, the runaway slave, back to Philemon as required by law." But that is not how Paul saw the situation. Instead he writes, "I am sending Onesimus, our faithful and beloved brother, who is one of you." One commentator described it this way:

> The apostle recommends Onesimus to the brethren in Colosse, as a "faithful and beloved brother, who is one of you," and he goes on to say that Tychicus and Onesimus will make known to them all things that have happened to Paul in Rome. Such a commendation would greatly facilitate Onesimus's return to Colosse. But Paul does more. He furnishes Onesimus with a let-

ter written by himself to Philemon. Returning to a city where it was well known that he had been neither a Christian nor even an honest man, he needed someone to vouch for the reality of the change which had taken place in his life. And Paul does this for him both in the Epistle to the Colossians and in the letter to Philemon. [ISBE]

Now, at the end of this verse Paul says that **they** – both Tychicus and Onesimus – "will inform you about the whole situation here." Both men were designated messengers to the church at Colossae. Paul will now mention some of his other companions in ministry.

Col 4:10 - Aristarchus, my fellow prisoner, sends you his greetings; and also Barnabas's cousin Mark (about whom you received instructions; if he comes to you, welcome him);

Several people remained with Paul in Rome, and in this verse Paul mentions two of them. Aristarchus was one of Paul's constant companions. We know that he originally came from Thessalonica (Acts 20:4), so he probably became a believer during Paul's second missionary journey around ten years prior to Paul's letter to the Colossians. It seems that Aristarchus traveled with Paul from that point onward. He was one of the believers who was seized by the Ephesian mob during the riot stirred up by the silversmiths (Act 19:29), and he was one of the men who accompanied Paul from Greece to Jerusalem with the collection for the churches in Judea (Act 20:4). He is next mentioned as accompanying Paul to Rome (Act 27:2) where he assisted Paul and shared in his imprisonment. Aristarchus had a habit of being with Paul during difficult times. He must have been of tremendous help to the aging apostle.

Barnabas' cousin Mark is none other than John Mark who wrote the Gospel of Mark. Paul traveled with Barnabus and Mark on their first missionary journey together from Antioch in Syria to Cyprus and southern Asia Minor (Acts 13:5). Even though Paul had a falling out with both Barnabas and Mark at that time (Act 13:13; 15:36-39), Paul was writing his Colossian letter almost 15 years later, and during the intervening years Mark had more than proven himself in Christian ministry. As one commentator said, "The man Paul once rejected became one of his greatest helpers." [MacArthur, 195]

Here Paul writes to the Colossians that they had already "received instructions" about Mark, and that "if he comes to" then they are to "welcome him." Mark truly is an important minister and servant of Christ at this time in Church history.

Col 4:11 - and also Jesus who is called Justus; these are the only fellow workers for the kingdom of God who are from the circumcision, and they have proved to be an encouragement to me.

Paul now mentions Jesus who is called Justus as his third companion. This is the only place in the New Testament where he is mentioned, so we know very little about him. The reason these three men were named together is because they are all Jewish believers. As Paul says, they are fellow workers **who are from the circumcision**. They all share a common Jewish heritage, and they all have suffered similar persecutions from the Jews as they declared "this mystery among the Gentiles, which is Christ in you, the hope of glory." (Col 1:27).

When Paul says they are **fellow workers for the kingdom of God** he is being consistent with how he used the term kingdom previously in Col 1:13. There he stated that God "rescued us from the domain of darkness, and transferred us to the kingdom of His beloved Son." Just as God makes believers legal heirs of a heavenly inheritance which we do not possess now but will ultimately receive in the future (Col 1:12), so He also guarantees the legal status of believers as members of Christ's future kingdom. They will ultimately enter into the kingdom of God to enjoy their inheritance, and they are working diligently to give others that same opportunity.

At the end of this verse Paul says that his Jewish Christian companions have been a great **encouragement to me**. As we recall from the last chapter, the very reason that Paul had been imprisoned was because the Jews reacted violently to his presentation of the gospel. So it makes sense that Paul would be encouraged to have some of his Jewish brothers as brothers in Christ too. Not all Jews rejected Jesus the Messiah, but a few of them believed and became members of the body of Christ, the Church.

Col 4:12 - Epaphras, who is one of your number, a bondslave of Jesus Christ, sends you his greetings, always laboring earnestly for you in his prayers, that you may stand perfect and fully assured in all the will of God.

Paul now goes on to name some of his Gentile companions. We have already met Epaphras in the first chapter of Colossians, where Paul said they "heard the word of truth, the gospel which has come to you, just as in all the world also it is constantly bearing fruit and increasing, even as it has been doing in you also since the day you heard of it and understood the grace of God in truth, just as you learned it from Epaphras" (Col 1:5-8). He was the one who first shared the gospel message with the people of his home town, and when many of his neighbors believed in Christ, Epaphras then spent time carefully teaching them the truths of the faith.

Paul described him as a "beloved fellow bond-servant, who is a faithful servant of Christ on our behalf" (Col 1:7). Then here in this verse Paul confirms that Epaphras was from Colossae, but that he did not return home carrying this letter to the Colossians. Instead he remained in Rome with Paul, and while he was there he carried on an important prayer ministry for all those in the Lycus Valley.

When Paul said Epaphras was "always **laboring earnestly** for them in his prayers" he used the Greek word *agōnizomai* from which we get our English word "agonizing." This is the same word that Paul had used in Col 1:29 to describe his own efforts in ministry, and Epaphras' prayer is almost identical to what Paul said that he was praying for the Colossians in Col 1:9-12.

Col 4:13 - For I testify for him that he has a deep concern for you and for those who are in Laodicea and Hierapolis.

Paul now gives first-hand testimony to the passion of Epaphras for all the believers in the Lycus Valley. **Concern** is the Greek word *ponos* which can be translated as "anguish or intense desire." Since Epaphras was the founder of these churches, he took on a great burden to pray for them and to work tirelessly for their spiritual growth. We see here that both of the major cities in the Lycus Valley are mentioned, so Epaphras' original message and influence has spread throughout the area. There were now groups of believers in all three of the towns in the valley.

Col 4:14 - Luke, the beloved physician, sends you his greetings, and also Demas.

Next Paul mentions Luke, who would write the Gospel of Luke and the book of Acts. He accompanied Paul on his second missionary journey a decade previously (Acts 16:10), and Luke became a beloved companion throughout the rest of Paul's life (2 Tim 4:11). Here we see that Luke was a physician, and he probably tended to Paul's medical needs as well as assisting in the ministry work.

Demas is mentioned here only by name, but Philemon 1:24 includes him among Paul's fellow laborers. All we know about him is that he eventually deserted Paul and returned to Thessalonica, having loved worldly things more than the

Lord's work (2 Tim 4:10).

Col 4:15 - Greet the brethren who are in Laodicea and also Nympha and the church that is in her house.

Paul also sends his greetings to the believers who are in Laodicea, as well as to Nympha and the church that meets in her house. This is the only mention of Nympha, so we have no other information about her or the believers who worshiped together in her home. At this time in church history there were no purpose-built meeting halls for believers like there were synagogues for the Jews. Christian fellowships would typically meet in members' homes. One commentator expressed it this way: "We must remember that there was no such thing as a special Church building until the third century. Up to that time the Christian congregations met in the houses of those who were the leaders of the church." [Barclay in Guzik] It is possible that fellowships of believers in the Lycus Valley also shared teaching pastors.

Col 4:16 - When this letter is read among you, have it also read in the church of the Laodiceans; and you, for your part read my letter that is coming from Laodicea.

Paul then made some requests about how his letters should be circulated among the churches. First he says that after the Colossians have publicly read and studied this letter, then they are to send it to the neighboring church in Laodicea. This would have been an easy way for Paul's teaching to impact several fellowships without requiring him personally to be present.

Next Paul asks that the Colossians also publicly read and study the letter that is coming from Laodicea. Some have assumed that Paul wrote a special letter to the Laodiceans which has since been lost, but it is more likely that Paul is referring to the letter to the Ephesians. One commentator explained it this way: "It is well-nigh certain that Ephesians was a circulating letter meant to be exchanged among the Churches of Asia. It may be that this circulating letter had reached Laodicea and was now on the way to Colosse." [Barclay in Guzik]

Some of the earliest manuscripts of the book of Ephesians do not have the words "in Ephesus" in the first verse, and the early Church fathers were familiar with a copy of that letter which was kept at Laodicea. Textual scholars of the New Testament have determined that most of the available manuscripts were copies of the one kept in Ephesus, so it came to be called the Epistle to the Ephesians. We know that Tychicus carried both of these letters on his journey from Paul in Rome to Ephesus, Laodicea, and Colossae (Eph 6:21). So it is probably best to think of this so-called "missing" letter as a circulating letter delivered first to Ephesus and then to Laodicea before it would eventually reach Colossae. The exchange of important teaching materials like this was the common procedure among the churches.

Col 4:17 - Say to Archippus, "Take heed to the ministry which you have received in the Lord, that you may fulfill it."

Last of all Paul addresses Archippus. He is mentioned only here and in the letter to Philemon. The way he is included in that letter may imply that Archippus was the son of Philemon since he is mentioned in the context of the wife of Philemon (Apphia) and his household. The context here in Col 4:17, coming immediately after the mention of the church is Laodicea, has led some to think that he may have been the minister of the church there. This side of heaven, there is no way to know for certain, but clearly Paul valued Archippus as a **fellow soldier** (*sustratiōtēs*) for the cause of Christ. One commentator has said:

In Philemon 1:2 he is mentioned by Paul as his "fellow-soldier," and it is evident that the apostle meant to speak of him with honor. There is no evidence, as has been supposed by some, that he intended to imply that Archippus had been remiss in the performance of his duties, but the apostle doubtless meant to encourage him and to excite him to further zeal in the work of the Lord. [Barnes]

Paul's command to Archippus is to take heed or watch diligently to be engaged in the ministry to which he was called. He uses the Greek verb *plēroō* in the present tense to say, "keep on filling it full." Paul intends to encourage him in the work he has taken on for the Church.

Col 4:18 - I, Paul, write this greeting with my own hand. Remember my imprisonment. Grace be with you.

In this final verse, Paul himself takes the pen to sign the letter with his own hand and to share two last thoughts. First he says (literally), "Remember my chains." As one commentator expressed it, "Paul's reference to his chains is not a plea for sympathy; they are his claim to authority and the guarantee of his right to speak." [Barclay in Guzik] Another has said: "The chain clanked afresh as Paul took the pen to sign the salutation." [RWP] Yet another stated: "The clumsy handwriting was accounted for by the weight of the fetters on the poor wrists, yet his heart was full of love and joy." [Meyer]

Finally Paul scrawled, "grace be with you." He began this letter desiring grace for them and he ends on the same note, so God's grace are the bookends for all of his thoughts in between. As one commentator said, "May you still possess the favor and blessing of our Lord Jesus Christ. The apostle ends as he began. Without the grace of Christ they could not have become a Church; without this grace they could not continue to be one." [Clarke in e-Sword]

As we close our study, let's recall the words to the famous hymn:

> Wonderful grace of Jesus, Greater than all my sin,
> How shall my tongue describe it? Where shall His praise begin?
> Taking away my burden, Setting my spirit free,
> For the wonderful grace of Jesus reaches me.

www.ingramcontent.com/pod-product-compliance
Lightning Source LLC
Chambersburg PA
CBHW070850050426
42453CB00012B/2120